Sermons for Sermon Haters

Andre Papineau

Resource Publications, Inc.
San Jose, California

Other books by Andre Papineau
Breakthrough: Stories of Conversion
Jesus on the Mend: Healing Stories for Ordinary People
Biblical Blues: Growing Through Setups and Letdowns
Lightly Goes the Good News
Let Your Light Shine

Editorial Director: Kenneth Guentert
Managing Editor: Elizabeth J. Asborno
Copy Editor: Anne M. McLaughlin
Cover Design: George Collopy

Reprint Department
Resource Publications, Inc.
160 E. Virginia St., Suite 290
San Jose, CA 95112-5876

Library of Congress Cataloging in Publication Data
Papineau, Andre, 1937-
    Sermons for sermon haters / Andre Papineau.
        p.   cm.
    Includes index.
    ISBN 0-89390-229-2
    1. Catholic Church—Sermons. 2. Sermons, American.
    I. Title.
    BX1756.P337S4   1992
    252—dc20   91-48019

96 95 94 93 92 | 5 4 3 2 1

For Ed Gallowitz,
The Host of Midtown Manhattan.

My thanks to Dan Pekarske for his encouragement
and assistance in putting this book together.

Contents

II.
So What's the Problem?

III.
Preaching Jesus

IV.
Feastday Fanfare

Keeping Sight of the Familiar

Introduction

Sermon haters? C'mon! Why would anyone hate sermons?

Why? For starters, sermon haters hate sermons when they hear about:

> a Jesus who is a know-it-all: knew what his mother knew before she knew it; knew what was in the minds and hearts of everybody he met; knew the day and hour he'd die; knew the way he'd die and the way he'd rise;

> a Jesus who had a burning, obsessive desire to suffer and die his whole life long because that's what his dad wanted most for him;
> a Jesus who belonged to a holy trio, a family that never had any spats and differences with one another;

> a Jesus who was deadly serious: about life; about death; about life after death; and never ever exercised a laugh muscle;

1

a Jesus who spent all of his time and time off
exhorting people: to pray and pray some more;
to believe and believe some more; to eschew
their wicked ways and eschew some more; to
suffer endlessly and suffer others endlessly;

a Jesus who: winked at temptation; sweat only
once—in a garden; never put his arm around a
woman's shoulder; went to parties just to make
"Amen, Amen" pronouncements and win points
against his dumb opponents; never went to the
bathroom; never had any inner struggles—no
shadow problems as defined by C.G. Jung.

No reason for hating sermons? You've gotta be
kidding! But in case the oft-preached portrait of Jesus
that I have described isn't reason enough for hating
sermons, consider how preachers alienate congregations
when the sermons become occasions for chastising and
correcting them.

How many times have congregants heard harangues
about an evil people who do evil things in an evil world?
How often have people left the church feeling burdened
by sin, not affirmed to effect change in their lives? Why
is it that preaching has come to mean being preachy,
and delivering a sermon as sermonizing, if not because
preaching sermons has too often degenerated into
moralizing? If ever a word was overused in the pulpit, it
is the word *should.*

We shouldn't do dirty things!
We shouldn't have dirty thoughts!
We shouldn't say dirty words!
We shouldn't make dirty faces!
We should be humble!

2

We should be grateful!

We should be obedient!

We should honor our parents, our grandparents, and the pope!

"We should" is the club preachers wield in the pulpit to bully people into submission because the preached news sounds more bad than good, and who's going to embrace change based on bad news?

However, sermon haters are not only repelled by a world-denying, oppressive, guilt-inflicting approach to preaching, they are also insulted by an assault on their intelligence from well-intentioned likable preachers. Too quickly some preachers offer solutions to problems when they haven't really acknowledged and explored the problem under consideration. "Love your enemy!" "Forgive your betrayer!" "Just have faith!" If it were all that simple, everybody would have loved their enemies, forgiven their betrayers, and had oodles of faith before they entered the church doors. By not even identifying the tangle in relationships that give rise to problems of love, forgiveness, and faith, preachers are no longer struggling pilgrims journeying with their brothers and sisters. They see no difficulties, raise no questions, and find no complexities. They have arrived! The trouble is people do have problems that aren't so easily resolved, and they have questions for which there seem to be no simple answers. Much of the time, they see through a glass darkly, as St. Paul phrased it. And unless the preacher can see, hear, feel, and taste life as the people in the pews see, hear, feel, and taste it, then what the preacher says is irrelevant.

"Irrelevant" is an overused, abused word, but it is the most appropriate adjective when we think of words that preachers bandy about without explanation and assume everybody else finds meaningful. Such an assumption is yet another reason sermon haters hate sermons. What are preachers thinking when they load their sermons with words like grace, redemption, salvation, and sin? Simply because these are time-honored words doesn't mean they aren't time-conditioned! I'd like to know what associations people make with the word *grace*? I've heard of grace under pressure, a grace note and graceful gestures. Does the use of this word in common parlance help or hinder the preacher who speaks about grace from the pulpit? And what about the word *spirit* or *spiritual*? Do these words convey a sense of what is other-worldly? Is that what the preacher intends? What about *redemption*? For some people, Green Stamp redemption centers have more meaning!

And what about the use of images from the bible? Like shepherd, sheep, king, kingdom of God, father, and the body of Christ? Can we assume that everybody is deeply moved by being cast in the role of the sheep? Does the image of father appeal to all men and women in the congregation? Or are some people possibly repelled because of negative experiences with their father? Does the idea of kingship strike a chord in the hearts of people in the United States of America?

Preachers can take for granted that everybody is familiar with the meaning of certain holy days. Ask someone what the Immaculate Conception conjures up in their minds. White sheets? Have you ever heard of an annunciation outside the Feast of The Annunciation? And what about the Ascension? Up, up, and away! If those who are preaching don't critically examine how they are using these images, then their unexamined use means they either become irrelevant or what is worse, obnoxious! They are precious words because they come to us from our tradition, but unless preachers breathe life into them, they are no more than heirlooms—nice to look at on a rainy day.

Maybe what disturbs sermon haters most is what appears to be a given for preachers: namely, that there is some kind of invisible divide between themselves and the congregation. God is on the preachers' side of the divide and it is their business to bring God to the godless people on the other side. If they don't bridge the divide, the poor souls on the other side are in trouble. Maybe this attitude is the reason some preachers never seem to be able to finish a sermon. If they don't explain and explain their explanation, how can the others across the great divide be saved?

The I-alone-am-close-to-God mentality may also be the reason why preachers seem to know God's will so well. "God is asking us to..." or "God wants..." sounds like the preacher has nudged Jesus off to the side and is now sitting at the right hand of God himself!

Justifiably, sermon haters probably think that if God really is everywhere, there is no divide. And that the preacher would do everybody a service if he let it be known that the only reason he is preaching is to assure everyone God never left the scene, never could and never would—that he'd just like to celebrate God's continued presence with them. This message alone might be a reason some sermon haters might reconsider their aversion to sermons. If there is a problem many of us have, it is that we all tend to forget God is always with us, even when we think we're on our way to hell.

After all, what is hell but the illusion that we are
eternally separated from God?

There are many more reasons why sermon haters
hate sermons, many of which have to do with the
performance dimension—that is, the way the preacher
presents himself or herself: overbearing, pompous,
wooden, etc. Too much visual and verbal static can drive
people crazy—and right out the church door forever!

I think I have given enough reasons to make the point
that sermon haters are not mean-spirited persons who
have nothing better to do than sit around and bad
mouth preachers.

Having assumed the position of unofficial
spokesperson for sermon haters, I now find myself in
the unenviable position of offering sermon haters
sermons that I have written and delivered. Certainly I
realize the danger in which I have placed myself. And I
wish to minimize that danger by proposing what I do
and do not intend to do in the following sermons.

I realize the importance of narrative theology and its
impact on preaching in the form of the story sermon or
homily. So convinced am I of this form of preaching that
I have written five volumes of story sermons. The
reaction to these sermons has been favorable, and I
recommend that readers interested in the sermon as
story read any one of these books. Because I have
already written several stories elsewhere, I will not
present any in this volume.

The sermons in this book are categorized as sermons
that illustrate the following: exploring a central image
or expression; respecting the problematic in life;
preaching a thoroughly human Jesus; identifying the
simply human in the extraordinary events celebrated on

feastdays. Accordingly, this book is arranged in four parts with introductory comments.

I know that I expose myself to the kind of critique I have given regarding others' sermons. I welcome the critique because a healthy dialogue between the preacher and the congregation is an important step in gaining at least a grudging respect from sermon haters who have been subjected over and over to long-winded monologues. Even grudging respect from a sermon hater would make this preacher happy!

I.

Images Then and Now

Connecting Past and Present Through the Image

Then and now. Now and then. Not simply then, not simply now, but then and now. Then is the past and now is the present. Then is the biblical story, and now is ours. If we get lost in the biblical world and forget our own, we end up with archaeological excursions, historical memorabilia, and ho-hums from the congregation. However, if we forget the biblical world and concentrate on ours, horizons narrow to "my" little story and maybe yours without any reference to the Story that gives meaning to all our stories. Sermon haters are bored equally by irrelevant travelogues into the past and true confessions in the present.

The challenge is to relate then to now, and now to then. Frequently, the bridge between the two is a word, an image, a symbol, or an expression which is situated in either of these worlds but which no longer has any impact because it hasn't been employed to connect the two. Depending on which of the worlds we place ourselves in, we consider how the image functions in the one and how it can be appropriated in the other. By exploring the use of the image in both worlds, we are capable of discovering more meaning in both worlds.

For example, mud is an image in the story of the man born blind. First we consider its healing function and the frequent use of the word "mud"in the biblical story. This, in turn, leads us to recall the various uses of the word in our own world: "Here's mud in your eye," "muddying the waters," "clear as mud," "mudslinging." We then bring our understanding of the word from our world to the biblical world, where further reflection aids us in seeing new meaning in the biblical story. Through this process, we gain insight into this story not only as a story about healing but about mudslinging by those persons who wanted to discredit Jesus. Moreover, we learn that the mudslinging triggers the blind man to witness to his belief in Jesus. By using mud as a central image or symbol in the sermon, we can connect our world and the biblical world.

The intensive and extensive use of an image, a symbol, or an expression in a sermon often creates a cognitive and affective impact that the congregation would not otherwise experience. Initially, the image is just an image, but by the end of the sermon, it *is* the sermon because it sums up all that the sermon is about.

Part I is divided into two sections. The first section, entitled "A Word from the Sriptures to Us," consists of six sermons that use an image drawn from the biblical text in order to discover connections with our experiences. The second section, entitled "A Word from Us to the Scriptures," contains six sermons that explore a word or expression drawn from our "street talk" to illumine the text's meaning.

A Word
from the Scriptures to Us

Moment
of Glory

John 13:31-35

Once Judas had left, Jesus said: "Now is the Son of
Man glorified: and God is glorified in him. (If God has
been glorified in him,) God will, in turn, glorify him
in himself, and will glorify him soon."

*T*he word "glory" occurs frequently in the readings for
today's liturgy. In the gospel Jesus tells us that he
glorifies his Father and his Father glorifies him. We are
so familiar with the meaning of the word "glory" that we
might miss the startling way in which Jesus uses the
word. I think it is important to consider how we use the
word and how Jesus does because what he says may
prove helpful to us in difficult times.

First, I hope that everyone here has experienced a
moment of glory—a moment when you really come
alive, when you are glad to be you and doing what you
are doing. Let's say that you score the winning point in
a basketball game. That's a glory moment. Or maybe

you bake a loaf of bread that is as high as the sky.
That's another glory moment. Or you graduate with
highest honors from high school or college. Another
glory moment! Maybe you sing a song or run a race like
you've never sung or ran before. Those are glory
moments.

Glory moments don't occur often, but when they do
they are worth savoring and remembering. Of course,
glory moments wouldn't even be if you had no one to
share those moments with. So you bake a loaf of bread
as high as the sky but no one is there to say, "Wow!" Or
you make the winning point and there is dead silence in
the bleachers. You graduate with honors in the
auditorium but mom and dad are at home watching TV.
How would you feel without others to share those
moments? How would you feel if others ignored or
laughed at you in your glory moments? Lonely or silly or
ashamed or angry?

Yet, is it possible that even these tragic moments,
these moments of shame, can reveal a new kind of
glory? Is it possible that a person going through a
divorce can discover glory in that process? Is it possible
that a man or woman who discovers and acknowledges
that he or she is an alcoholic can find glory in that
discovery? Can the unmarried girl who finds herself
pregnant discover glory even here? Can we go further
and say that an old person whom others ignore can also
discover glory?

I think so. Because when Jesus speaks of God's glory,
he is not talking about his "high" moments when he
heals, or when he mesmerizes the crowds with his
preaching. No, he is talking about his shameful death
by crucifixion. He is talking about the moment when he

is regarded as a common criminal pinned to a cross. He is saying that the moment of death is the moment when God's glory is present as it has never been present before. God is fully alive in Jesus' moment of pain. In this brokenness and shame, God comes to life and pours that life out through Jesus.

And what does this tell us? It tells us that whenever we experience moments of shame, these moments might also be God's glory moments in us. We might be dead as a doornail; we might feel empty and lifeless; we might be ready to give up—want to hide under a rug or climb a tree; we might want to close the doors and not talk to anybody. But in those moments, God comes alive and shines in our brokenness. And don't ever forget this! The glory of God doesn't depend on how well we shine or strut or sing or run or bake bread. No, all we need to know is that Jesus has turned this whole thing around. The tragic moments can bear the glory of God. Amen. Amen.

Let us pray, brothers and sisters, that when we are tempted to give up, there is a God waiting to reveal his glory in us if we do but believe. Amen. Amen. Glory, glory, glory!

Is There Dirt
in the Kingdom?

Mark 4:1-20

"But those sown on good soil are the ones who listen
to the word, take it to heart, and yield at thirty- and
sixty- and a hundredfold."

*I*s there dirt in the Kingdom? That's what I need to
know. My question isn't an idle one. Nor is it an
invitation to a dispassionate discussion on whether
there is or isn't dirt. No, the answer to this question has
serious consequences, which I am willing to sit down
and discuss—later. But first I must know: is there dirt
in the kingdom? Anywhere in the Kingdom? Is there
dirt in heaven?

I fear there isn't! I have been told that the streets are
paved with gold and that the gates of heaven are made
of mother-of-pearl. Very clean, wouldn't you say? Not a
word about dirt. Sounds to me like heaven is Crystal
Cathedral! I am getting anxious. I imagine myself
arriving at the heavenly gates where Mr. Clean is

standing guard. He approaches me, sizes me up from
head to foot, and with a look of disapproval says, "Hey
man! You can't come in here. Look at your shoes—dirt
on the soles! No dirty soles allowed here. And look at
those fingernails! Dirty! Dirty! What's more, you
got—you got ring around the collar! Look buddy, this is
heaven; we are spiritual, spi-ri-tual! Understand? Go
back down to earth! That's where dirt belongs, down,
down, down!"

Well, now I am really beginning to worry. If there's no
dirt in the upper Kingdom, will I find it in the lower? I
hesitate to say it, but I don't think I will find it there
either. Why? Because dirt doesn't have such a hot
reputation here either. We talk about dirty old men; we
get hot and bothered about people with dirty mouths
and dirty minds. People who mess up their underwear
we describe as having soiled themselves. "On earth as it
is in heaven," clean is in. We think clean is great! We
like clean-cut people who keep their slates clean. Even
white-collar crimes don't sound so bad because they are
clean sounding. And we have an expression that sums
up our veneration for clean: cleanliness is next to
godliness. Now this really tells us where a lot of folk
find the Kingdom, doesn't it? So what chance does dirt
have? Not much if people like Mr. Clean and the Tidy
Bowl man have anything to say about it! So I guess
there is no dirt in the Kingdom.

But wait! I have forgotten something! I have forgotten
about Jesus' parable on the Kingdom, that parable
about the sower who goes out to sow seed.

Well I'll be! This is news, startling, revolutionary,
good news! About the Kingdom and dirt! Where does
the seed land? Where does it flourish? Where does God's

Is There Dirt in the Kingdom?

word take root? In the *dirt!* Not cleaned up, sterile sand, but dirt, dirty dirt! Make no mistake! That seed grows in dirty dirt! And do you know what makes up dirty dirt? Old fish heads, rotten vegetables, moldy fruit, and ding dong dung! Phewww! That's where the seed goes. That's where the word goes. It doesn't take root on the surface, in what is cleannn and superficial, not in what is polite and polished. No, it can't live there. It withers and dies there. It needs to go into the shadowy interiors, into the smelly regions, into shadowlands. That is where it is transformed and grows. And what is that dirty dirt? Where in the Kingdom do we find it?

It is us. In us, the us we want to hide, the us we want to sweep under the carpet of our lives. It is what we regard as the crap of our lives—everything we fear and regard as negative or unseemly about ourselves. That is the dirty dirt. But it is here that God's word thrives—in the manure pile. Did you ever see flowers blossom in the manure? I have. Imagine! Salvation in a dung heap! We don't need to be scrubbed from top to bottom before receiving God's word. We don't need to be clean all over. All we need to do is let the word in, into the dirt, deep, deep down.

Is there dirt in the Kingdom? There sure is! And we're all standing in it right now.

Remember this: The Compost Heap of today is the Garden of God tomorrow!

Going
to Seed

Mark 4:1-20

"Some seed, finally, landed on good soil and yielded grain that sprang up to produce at a rate of thirty- and sixty- and a hundredfold."

I don't know if you have ever considered the fact that the seeds which the sower scatters have a history prior to their being scattered. By this I mean that the seeds had a past, were developing into something and then turned into seeds again before being thrown into the ground. If we can speak to that history and reflect on it, perhaps we shall be able to appreciate the parable of the sower and the seed in a new way, that is, we shall be able to understand the parable as a story of transformation or conversion.

I hold before me a beautiful apple, shiny, ripe, mature as an apple could be. It is fully developed. In Apple Land the other apples might admire and envy it because it has become such a success at being an apple.

So what further development could we expect of this
apple?
What is going to happen to it? Unless someone eats it,
it is going to get rotten, deteriorate, break down and go
to seed. I wasn't able to find a rotten apple to illustrate
my point. That is too bad because apples headed for skid
row aren't nice to look at and they don't seem to have
any future whatsoever! They go to seed and become
seedy. Ugh! Who likes seedy apples? Who likes peachy
peaches that have degenerated into pulpy peaches and
then into puckered-out peaches? Or melons that get
mushy? So by the time the apple has gone to seed, it
appears to be at the end of the line—good for nothing!
But lo and behold! At the point when it becomes seed,
it is taken up by the sower, some Johnnie Appleseed,
and thrown into the soil. There the seed deteriorates.
But here—at its lowest point—a reversal sets in. The
breakup of the apple, which led to its breaking down
into seed and further deterioration in the soil, now
means a breakthrough to new life! In the strangest way,
it is regenerated.
We too have a history similar to that of any other
seed. We develop, mature, ripen, grow, have a future.
Counselors, therapists, spiritual directors, moderators,
mentors, psychotherapists, gurus, parents, siblings, and
friends cultivate our maturing. They encourage us to
realize our potential and get us to self-actualize. That is
good; it is encouraging. But you know, there may be a
time when all that ripening, all that maturing, all that
self-actualizing and all that polishing has to give way to
some kind of breaking up and breaking down if there is
to be any breakthrough to something new and vital.

There may be a time when it is necessary for us to experience ourselves as falling apart, as reaching our limits, as feeling fragmented—as going to seed. And yes, as even appearing seedy to ourselves and others. This is necessary if transformation is to take place in our lives. Going to seed is paradoxically part of the process of growth and transformation. We experience a dismemberment and then we are cast into the ground where it is dark. Our experience of the darkness we may call disillusionment or depression or despair or all three of these combined. But it is in the dark night of the dark soil that we undergo the transformation which brings us to a new lease on life and a new way of understanding ourselves.

So, you see, the story of the sower of seeds is the story of all of us who are words coming from God that need to undergo transformation. And transformation means acknowledging that some kind of putrefaction or breaking down needs not only to be endured but to be embraced if any kind of growth is to take place.

Sheep or Shepherd?

John 10:1-10

"The one who enters through the gate is shepherd of the sheep; the keeper opens the gate for him. The sheep hear his voice as he calls his own by name and leads them out. When he has brought out (all) those that are his, he walks in front of them, and the sheep follow him because they recognize his voice."

"*I* am the shepherd; you are the sheep." Even before the words are out, I want to say "No! No! I'm nobody's sheep!" I hate being assigned the role of sheep, even if it is Jesus who is the shepherd. Why am I so resistant?

For starters, the Greek word for "sheep" is *proboton,* which means "the forward walking animal." Great! Sheep all move together in the same direction—forward. Get them going forward and they can't go in reverse or sideways. No wonder I admire the black sheep in the herd. Maybe he gets lost but at least there's something unique and different about this sheep. However, my

problem with sheep isn't limited to their locomotive
pattern.

We have a couple of expressions that suggest our real
feelings about sheep. When someone is unclear in his
thinking, we say he is wooly-minded. And what do we
say of someone who has been swindled? She's been
fleeced! What word do we choose to describe someone
who has made a boo-boo and looks it? Sheepish, of
course! Talk about fanciful day dreamers and you're
talking about wool-gatherers! Not only do sheep seem to
be pretty dumb they are also pretty smelly. Get a whiff
of them some day and you'll understand why I have
such a resistance to identifying with sheep.

No, if I'm going to play a role in this shepherd-sheep
scenario...well, move over Jesus! I want to be the
shepherd. Shepherds are caring souls. Caring is
tending, looking after, nurturing. This is someone who
cares; gives direction to the lost and wooly-minded;
takes the initiative in reaching out to others; accepts
those who do dumb things and doesn't judge them. I've
known a lot of shepherds, and some of the best are
people whom we never call shepherds. Bartenders come
to mind. They tend more than bars; they tend souls by
listening to them hours on end. And there are the
nurses' aides in hospitals—more good listeners who
aren't fired up with all kinds of advice for those in their
care.

Yes, I'd like to be a shepherd, someone who is a giver,
someone who operates from a position of strength. What
do you say to that, Jesus?

I can hear Jesus laughing, and I think I know why. If
you're going to be a "good" shepherd, you had better be
in touch with the inner dumb sheep you want to

disclaim and leave behind. After all, if we are tending those who are lost and confused, then we had better be in touch with where we are lost and wooly-minded. How else can we help others? If we are tending those who say and do dumb things, then we had better be in touch with the embarrassing things we have said and done. Sheep are vulnerable and capable of being wounded. And unless the shepherd is in touch with that, he or she will be of no help to those sheep.

So maybe Jesus won't mind my identifying with the shepherd provided I am willing to acknowledge that I am also a sheep. Only then can I be a shepherd to others and discover in my own confusion the Good Shepherd as well as the sheep in them.

Heart attack leading killer
Cardiologist a American Heart Assoc
(gained certain changes)
regular exercise
watch our died, etc
They warn us. of the various signs

A Matter
of Heart

Joel 2:12-18

Yet even now, says the LORD, return to me with your
whole heart, with fasting, and weeping, and mourn-
ing; Rend your hearts, not your garments, and return
to the LORD, your God. For gracious and merciful is
he, slow to anger, rich in kindness, and relenting in
punishment.

*T*oday is Ash Wednesday, and if we take to heart the
prophet Joel's admonition, we can see a correspondence
with another important day of the year—Valentine's
Day. What possible relationship is there between the
two? Today it's sackcloth and ashes; Valentine's Day it's
chocolates and roses. Ash Wednesday is a downer and
Valentines Day is an upper—at least for lovers. So what
could these two days have in common? The answer, in a
word, is *heart*. They are both days of the heart. And by
considering them together, they both gain in meaning.

It's clear why Valentine's Day is a day of the heart. It
is the day when hearts go out to one another. It

shouldn't be difficult to understand why Ash Wednesday is also a day of the heart. After all, we are called to conversion, which is a change of heart. As Joel puts it in the first reading "Even now says the Lord, return to me with your whole heart...Rend your heart, not your garments."

Ash Wednesday and Valentine's Day are more meaningful together when we consider the different contexts in which we use the word "heart." We speak about people who are hard-hearted or have hearts of stone, and we mean that these people are inflexible, rigid, and unyielding. There is no "give" in their personalities. They are resistant to change. Moreover, they are callous, indifferent, and insensitive to others' feelings. These people are aptly called Scrooges, Simon Legrees, and Hard-Hearted Hannahs.

Then there are the half-hearted souls who aren't really committed or involved in what they are doing. They are lukewarm, tepid. In all fairness to half-hearted people, we ought to point out that they may not be fully engaged in one area of their life but fully committed in another. Still, there are people whose overall attitude is half-hearted. They have never been passionately involved or committed to any cause or any person.

The downhearted are those who are depressed and sad. The causes for being downhearted are many. Someone has lost a job or friend or spouse and is downhearted. Maybe the person feels down on life and has lost interest altogether; he or she, too, is downhearted.

When we speak of broken-hearted persons, we are referring to people who frequently are like their downhearted counterparts. However, we are likely to associate the broken-hearted person with an aching, throbbing heart. People going through a breakup are subject to being broken-hearted. The breakup of a marriage, a romance, or a friendship comes to mind, but so too does someone's untimely death. Dashed hopes and expectations regarding the future might signal the advent of a broken heart.

Everyone knows what it is like to have a lonely heart. Loneliness can be so devastating that if it is intense and unrelieved, it can lead to premature death.

Hopefully, everyone here knows what it is like to have a full heart. People with full hearts are overwhelmed by another's generosity, and their hearts are brimming over with gratitude. Paradoxically, their hearts are so full that they can't find the words to express that fullness adequately. So, they stammer or remain silent because their hearts are so full. If half-hearted people are lukewarm in their commitments, whole- hearted persons are passionate in theirs. They give themselves *totally* to the task at hand, to the people in their lives, to life itself. They are also "whole"—that is, they are people of integrity. Their zest and energy is admirable!

There are other ways of speaking about the heart, but I think I have named enough of them to stimulate our thinking about Ash Wednesday and Valentine's Day and their relationship to one another.

We begin by reflecting on Joel's call to a change of heart or, as he describes it, a return of the heart. It seems to me that the change to which he invites us involves a change from being hard- hearted to being whole-hearted. The process begins with the acknowledgment that we are hard-hearted or have

hearts of stone in some areas of our lives. We are rigid
or inflexible in our attitudes toward certain people, or
we are unyielding in regard to certain attitudes,
opinions, and ideas which we have. However,
conversions don't take place simply because we
recognize our need to be converted.

We need to experience some kind of a breakup or
breakdown of the heart before the process is really
under way. For example, some people are entirely
devoid of compassion toward others who experience
marital problems until their own marriages are on the
rocks. Or they fail to understand why other parents
have problems with their children until they themselves
have similar problems. When they are broken, they
experience disillusionment. By this I mean that their
aspirations, dreams, and convictions about themselves,
others, and life no longer work as they did in the past.
They feel helpless and confused. Yet, it is precisely
because of the broken heart in which confusion reigns
that there is the possibility of change, of seeing in a new
way. It is also out of this brokenness that people who
earlier had little compassion experience a newfound
affinity with those persons whom they had previously
ignored. Now they are able to receive others' hearts and
they find their own hearts going out to others in ways
that surprise even themselves.

When the heart goes out to others, we witness the
crowning stage in the conversion process. The hardened
heart breaks down into the broken heart and the broken
heart is disposed to experience a breakthrough. This
breakthrough or turning point occurs as the person's
heart goes out to others. The result of this is that a

person is more committed, more passionately involved with others—more whole-hearted!

Conversion is not a once-and-for-all event, however. We need to undergo conversion repeatedly. The surprising thing is we discover in our repeated conversion experiences that we have an ever-expanding heart. The expanding heart is what conversion is all about. Conversions are heart-stretching exercises! Out of our conversions, our hearts reach out to more and more people. We look to Jesus as the exemplar or model whose heart embraced all and whose theme song could easily be, "You've got to have heart, miles and miles of heart." Jesus not only has heart, a heart of gold and endless miles of it, but he is all heart! And through our conversion experience, we too hope to have miles and miles of heart. Finally, our response to conversion is our heart-felt gratitude to the Father, who has brought about this change in us.

To experience the conversion of heart, which is what Joel calls us to do today, Ash Wednesday, means we are then prepared to let our hearts go out to others on Valentine's Day. These two days are for all of us a matter of heart.

The Good Shepherdess

John 10:1-10

"The one who enters through the gate is shepherd of the sheep; the keeper opens the gate for him. The sheep hear his voice as he calls his own by name and leads them out. When he has brought out (all) those that are his, he walks in front of them, and the sheep follow him because they recognize his voice."

Jesus is the Good Shepherd who knows those who are his by their name, and they place their confidence in him based on the way his voice sounds as he calls them. My question is: in what way do we hear our names called by the Good Shepherd so that we too develop trust in the sound of that voice?

What seems to me to be particularly striking is that our first and perhaps most important experience of the Good Shepherd is through a woman, not a man. In other words, it is the good shepherdess, our mother, that leaves a lasting impact on our lives.

31

How your mother called your name has determined to a great extent how you responded to all succeeding shepherds and shepherdesses. Let us say your name is Randy. "Randy, you are such a nice baby," Randy's mother would say over and over. Or "Randy, open up your mouth wide so that mama can give you a yummy apricot," or "Randy, mama wants to change your diapers for you." Even in embarrassing situations, you might hear mama being gentle. "Randy, Randy, don't play with yourself in front of the company" or "Randy, mama knows you have poopoo to give to grandma and grandma is happy about poopoo but let's put it away for now," or "Randy, mama knows you learned a new word from daddy but I want you to save it for when you get older." From time to time, mama might get excited and nervous and angry. "Randy, Randy, don't ever cross the street without looking both ways" or "Randy, Randy, don't ever play with that big knife again." Even then, however, you knew by the sound of her voice that she cared.

So when you got older and the shepherdess wasn't around calling you Randy or looking after you, your name was still OK to yourself. You might get in trouble and you might panic, but you knew that Randy wouldn't fall apart. The sound of mama, the first shepherdess, was there in the background like music. "Randy, it's OK!" And when others related to you and called you Randy, the name brought back those pleasant associations so that you could recognize through the first shepherdess the voice of the other shepherds.

Suppose, however, that the first shepherdess said in a nasty tone, "Randy, don't do that again! Randy, how many times have I told you to stop eating that way!

Randy, you're naughty; you're a bad boy. Randy, you're no good! Randy, mama will leave you and never come back if you don't obey. Randy, don't bother me; can't you see I don't want you around! You're a nuisance." Randy doesn't find the sound of the shepherdess' voice inviting or reassuring, nor does his own name sound very nice coming from her lips.

Maybe even worse, mama ignores Randy and never says his name. It is as though Randy isn't there. And Randy could grow up being nobody because for all practical purposes the first shepherdess didn't even know his name. She never used it. Finally, when Randy got bigger he'd feel so empty because he had never experienced someone caring enough early in life to either say his name lovingly or at all.

Could a change take place in Randy's life? It would take someone who cared enough to say, "Randy, I like you." If a person said it consistently, maybe Randy would begin to value himself. We can get a feel for what I'm talking about if we substitute our own name for Randy's and call to mind the times when out of nowhere someone said, "You're Bill" or "You're Sally." And you didn't think anybody knew you. Wow! The sound of your name coming from someone who knew you and recognized you! Just when it was a bad day for you, someone noticed you and said your first name. And by the sound of the person's voice, you knew that person genuinely cared—and for that moment became your good shepherd.

When we call one another by name and we care, we are in that moment being good shepherds in the tradition of Jesus and the first shepherdess, our mother. Oh, the sound of the voice. It means so much!

A Word
from Us to the Scriptures

Do You Know
What I Mean?

John 1:1-18

"In the beginning was the Word; the Word was in
God's presence, and the Word was God. He was present to God in the beginning. Through him all things
came into being, and apart from him nothing came to
be."

*F*or several years I have been intrigued by the first
chapter of John's gospel, especially verses 1-3: In the
beginning was the Word, and the Word was with God,
and the Word was God. He was in the beginning with
God. All things came to be through him, and without
him nothing came to be. What I understand by this is
that we, too, are words since we came into being
through the Word. We are words through the Word!
Now this idea might not seem interesting to you and it
didn't mean much to me until I began reflecting on it in
light of an expression we use in our conversations. We
use it so often that we are generally unaware we are

saying it until someone draws our attention to it. Do you know what I mean?

Have you figured out what expression I mean? Here's a hint: I've already used it. The expression is, "Do you know what I mean?" How many times a day do we sprinkle our conversations with these words? We want to make a point or chart a course of action or clarify a misunderstanding, and invariably we intersperse "Do you know what I mean?" throughout our explanations, proposals, clarifications, etc. Frequently, we don't even manage to get out all of the words. "D'ya know?" or "You know?" satisfies our need.

What is it we are asking when we say, "Do you know what I mean?" Certainly we are looking to another for some comprehension or understanding of the message we want to communicate. But I think more is involved. When I say, "Do you know what I mean?" I am asking someone if that person is able to grasp the meaning that *I* am. Do *I* make sense? Do *I* mean anything to you? On the other hand, when someone says to me, "I know what you mean," the other is acknowledging *me*. "I am with you; you are not alone." When someone receives my meaning and my meaning is *me*, not just what I happen to be saying, that person is receiving me. And it isn't until another person says "Yes, I know what you mean," that I know what I mean! In other words, I am more meaningful to myself when another person finds me meaningful. On the other hand, in my attempt to find out whether the other knows what I mean—and he or she doesn't—then I'm not sure what I mean!

When another person responds, "I know what you mean," he or she is providing feedback. This feedback clarifies who I am and what I am intending by mirroring the other person's understanding. Feedback also suggests that such a response is nourishing. I am fed and energized.

Our desire to find others who know what we mean is never ending because we always mean much more than we can ever express in words during any one exchange with others. Consequently, when someone impatiently says, "Say what you mean," we are frustrated because who we are—what we think and feel at the moment—means more than we can press out into words. What is important is that even if we can't say all that we mean, we mean what we say—that is, our words do not mislead or deceive. When we mean what we say, we want to speak ourselves into our words to the extent that this is possible.

We get a better grasp of the importance of finding others who know what we mean if we imagine ourselves to be in a foreign country where we have no knowledge of the language and the inhabitants have no knowledge of ours. We experience frustration, loneliness, and alienation because there is no one we know who can comprehend what we mean. Now it doesn't take much reflection to realize that you can be in your own home, neighborhood, city, or country and not find people who know what you mean, particularly if you've just been told you have a cancerous tumor, or you are going through a divorce, or you've lost someone through death. But when you do—when someone listens without judging, offering advice, lecturing, or moralizing—then the words "I know what you mean" provide some relief from bearing the burden alone.

You may be wondering what possible connection there is between what I have been discussing and my opening remark about the fact that we are all words through the Word. The connection is this. As personal words who have come into being through the Word, we are words whose meaning is derived from the meaningful word, the Word. Because we are meaning-filled words generated through the Meaningful Word, I think we are in search of our common parentage through the never-ending question we raise, "Do you know what I mean?" and the equally never-ending response we give to others, "I know what you mean." We are a community of words restlessly searching for our common origin. Our search is the search to find other words who understand our meaning and our receptivity is as words who receive others' meaning. In this reaching out and receiving (that is, through the "Do you know what I mean?" and "Yes, I know what you mean") we as a community become more aware of what we mean to each other, and therefore we mirror more adequately that Word through whom we all came to be. It is our dignity as meaningful words to be supportive of one another. And through this mutual support, we create a symphony of words praising the Word who is the love song forever sung by the One from the beginning.

Do you know what I mean?

Be Prepared

Luke 12:35-38

"Let your belts be fastened around your waists and your lamps be burning ready. Be like men awaiting their master's return from a wedding, so that when he arrives and knocks, you will open for him without delay. It will go well with those servants whom the master finds wide-awake on his return."

"*B*e prepared," Jesus tells his disciples. Be prepared for when the master returns. I can certainly appreciate his concern about being prepared for the Kingdom Day when it rolls around.

After all, if a person spends a lifetime snoozing, what's to keep him from snoring through the banquet on Kingdom Day? Who wants snorers in the Kingdom?

I can understand why Jesus would be cool toward some cat who was mean and cruel to the brothers and the sisters on earth. Would this person be prepared to be amiable and friendly as he sat next to someone at the table on Kingdom Day?

And I am one hundred percent behind Jesus when he tells us to keep our lights burning brightly lest we miss him when he comes on the night train to pack us all up for the ride to Kingdom Country.

Yes, I say "Amen! Amen!" to Jesus' apprehension about anybody who walks around like a zombie and doesn't seem to hear or see or care to hear or see what's happening in the world—ever! You don't want to have them as dinner partners for a banquet that's gonna last forever.

But after I had said my amens and agreed that we needed to be prepared, I think I'd discreetly draw Jesus aside—I would know better than to tell him what I had to say in front of the others —and I would suggest that he not push the preparation bit too hard. I'd gently ask him not to go overboard instructing us how important it is to be prepared.

Why? Because unlike the brothers and the sisters in the first century, we have been encouraged, cajoled, warned, and threatened to be prepared since our day one.

Keep your eyes open!
Pay attention!
Don't get caught with your pants down!
Look smart!
Keep your eyes on the road!
Stop daydreaming!
Put your money away for a rainy day!
Plan ahead!
Take notes!
Watch out for the guy next to you!
Or your wife!
Or your cat!

Isn't it the case that we admire people who are:

> alert,
> sharp as a tack
> don't trust *just* anybody
> have eyes in the back of their head
> don't let anything pass them by
> don't miss a trick.

Oh, we've been told to prepare all right! I would point out to Jesus that our problem is not that we haven't been asked to prepare but that we have been overly concerned with being prepared. Why? Because it is the way to manage and control our lives so nothing is left to chance or uncertainty. We don't want:

> surprises
> uninvited guests
> upheavals
> strangers at the doors
> last-minute notices
> to be caught off guard.

We want to say and do the right thing in the right place at the right time. But why do we feel we need to do away with all uncertainty? Why must we be in control?

Because if we are not prepared, if we are not in control, we will be done in, destroyed, overwhelmed by what lies in store. Preparation then turns into paranoia, a fear of what we can't control—the unpredictable!

But the unpredictable does happen. Life is full of surprises—and uncontrollable. It is frequently messy, muddy, murky. Attempts to reduce life to the manipulable are not only futile but also take the joy out of life.

For it is in those moments when we lose control and surrender ourselves that we are filled with awe and joy. We lose our breath at the sight of a beautiful sunset; we are taken up by someone's unexpected thoughtfulness; we are overwhelmed with gratitude at kindnesses bestowed. Ecstasy is losing ourselves and finding ourselves in communion with something larger than ourselves.

It is only when we are willing to surrender ourselves to whatever is happening that we are really prepared. Preparation is availability to the predictable and the unpredictable. It is the willingness to be surprised rather than the willfulness to control and do away with all surprise.

If we are too controlling, we shall miss out on the thousand-and-one ways in which the Kingdom comes to us. I want to tell you a little story that illustrates my point. A good friend of mine traveled with me through Europe a number of years ago. Whenever it was time to move on to another city, my friend would pack his belongings four hours ahead of time. You see, he wanted to be prepared. But invariably when it came time to go, he hastily unpacked everything because he had forgotten his ticket or some other item at the bottom of the bag. On one such occasion in Cologne, he carefully packed everything and commented as we walked on the street that he hadn't had to open his bag and that this time his preparation had paid off. At that very moment the strap on his bag broke, the bag fell to the ground and a bottle of a precious liqueur fell out, spilling onto the sidewalk. Within minutes the birds landed and slurped the liqueur—and I swear they chirped their way into the heavens tilting their wings as they had never done before. I must say that in that unpredictable moment my friend and I laughed into the heavens as the birds imaged for us in an instant what the kingdom must be like!

May we be prepared. But not so prepared that we miss the glory of God in the unpredictable.

Partners

Luke 10:25-37

On one occasion a lawyer stood up to pose him this
problem: "Teacher, what must I do to inherit everlasting life?" Jesus answered him: "What is written in the
law? How do you read it?" He replied: "You shall love
the Lord your God with all your heart, with all your
soul, with all your strength, and with all your mind;
and your neighbor as yourself." Jesus said, "You have
answered correctly. Do this and you shall live." But
because he wished to justify himself he said to Jesus,
"And who is my neighbor?"

"*W*ho is my neighbor?" A lawyer raised the question.
Smart lawyer! He wanted clarity, precision, accuracy!
Exactly who is the neighbor to be loved as one's self? He
needed to know the height, width, weight, and face of
the neighbor. Nothing was to be left to chance! Yes, he
was a smart lawyer, a sharp lawyer. But not smart
enough! The most important question he forgot to ask
was "Who or what is the *self* that we should love *as*?"

After all, if we don't know any dimensions of the self, then the clearest definition or description of who the neighbor is won't be very helpful. Love your neighbor as—as yourself. Who is that self? That's the big question.

What strikes me is how we always seem to regard the self as another person. We address it and refer to it as an inner other. For example, sometimes we don't get along with ourselves. And what do we say? "I don't like myself," or "I can't stand myself," or "I hate myself." Of course, if I feel this negatively toward myself, then I say "I can't go on living with myself."

At other times the way we talk betrays an uncertainty about the partner we call the self. We say "I'm afraid of myself," or "I don't know if I can trust myself," or "I don't know what got into myself."

Believe it or not, there are times when we can't even find ourselves! So we say "Gee, I'm out of touch with myself," or "I'm beside myself." What's frightening is when we can't seem to control ourselves, as in "I lost control of myself," or "I don't know what happened to myself—I just started crying!" Of course it isn't always frightening. The unexpected is sometimes welcome and we say, "I surprised myself! I didn't know I had it in me."

Or, nothing surprising happens and we say "I am bored with myself" followed by "And I don't want to go home and be by myself."

But we have every right to be proud of ourselves when we say "I've got to go and work this thing out by myself" and return elated because "I figured it out by myself!" Then we don't mind the quiet. "I enjoy being alone with myself. I really like myself!"

Finally, we all know that there is only one other self that we will be with until the day we die—my self. So we say with a certain urgency, "I've got to be able to live with myself," and that means at times "I've got to confront myself," or "I need to take stock of myself."

The self we so often glibly assume to know is a partner in dialogue. It can be as unpredictable, maddening, frightening, friendly, and elusive as any person we know—friend, lover, or spouse. Given the range of feelings and attitude we bring to the self, no wonder it's such a challenge to love ourselves—and therefore our neighbor as the self.

Simply learning who this self is, however, is never the same as loving that self. And we cannot love that self unless we enlist its support to help us. Partners are in dialogue with one another; they are mutually supportive. One partner doesn't carry the burden of the relationship. In the present instance this means, *I* alone can't shoulder the burden of acceptance. My partner, that is, my *self* and *I* both bear that responsibility. How might we do this?

I spoke about being out of touch with myself. By this I meant being out of touch with moods, fantasies, feelings, attitudes. Certainly it is important that I reach out and touch this dimension of the self. But I also need to give my *self* permission to touch me. I permit these feelings, moods, etc., to be. I don't force them; I receive them. I get close to them and they get close to me.

Sometimes I try to figure things out and I am exhausted. *I* do the trying and *I* do the working—to no avail! Maybe if I rest, my self will come to my assistance with clues, suggestions, and hints. These are the creative moments when I discover that solutions to problems surface without my *I* having done anything at all to produce them. We know the wisdom of that self when we say, "I think I'm trying too hard to solve this problem; I'll put it on the back burner!" To put a problem on the back burner is to let the self as the creative agent provide insights not available on the front burner.

Then there are the times when I am afraid or bored by myself. In these instances I regard that self as an inner alien or as an enemy, and I try to hide from the self through distractions, for example playing loud music, never permitting myself to be alone, etc. Maybe if I quiet down and get close to that self, I will discover that being alone with my self isn't all that bad. Moments of solitude can be refreshing.

I am sure all of us have experienced moments when we said or did things that seemed out of character. We blurted out angry words or we sobbed uncontrollably over some insignificant issue. Perhaps we had long neglected getting close to that self and finally noticed how it was hurting. Like any other hurting person, when the self hurts it needs to be noticed. And if the self has been unduly neglected, it will call attention to itself in any way that it can.

I think the burden of accepting ourselves is relieved considerably if we realize that self-love is a partnership. I am called to love my self, but my self reaches out in love to me as well. Realizing this mutual give and take, I can be more open to those moments when I don't need to do anything to experience acceptance. It just happens! I feel at one with my self—there is a genuine communion in which my self and I experience being partners to one another.

This partnership is essential if we are ever to reach out and accept our neighbor as ourselves. Without self-acquaintance and self-love, any relationships we establish with others will be extremely shallow because intimacy with others presumes intimacy with one's self.

You're Just
Too Good to be True

Mark 6:1-6

Jesus went to his own part of the country followed by
his disciples. When the Sabbath came he began to
teach in the synagogue in a way that kept his large
audience amazed. They said: "Where did he get all
this? What kind of wisdom is he endowed with? How
is it such miraculous deeds are accompanied by his
hands?"

> You're just too good to be true!
> Can't take my eyes off of you.
> You're just like heaven to touch;
> I want to hold you so much.
> At long last love has arrived,
> And I thank God I'm alive!

You're just too good to be true! You have a great build
and a sharp mind! You're a snappy dresser and a smart
looker. You've got all the credentials: sociable, tactful,
sensitive, caring. You're just too good to be true!

Sounds great, doesn't it? Wouldn't you be thrilled and overjoyed if someone approached you and marveled, "You're too good to be true!" That's how the home folks put it when they heard Jesus teach in the synagogue that Sabbath. As he taught they whispered, "Who's this dude? Where did he get all the smarts? How did he get the magic touch? He's better than a chiropractor or a shrink!" They went bananas over him! All lathered up they tripped over one another to get a better look. And when they did?

Someone in the crowd gasped, "That's that...ah...ah... Mary's kid, you know, the Mary who takes in the wash!" And someone else chimed in, "Sure, that's Mary's kid. Her husband is Joe, Joe whatchamacallit? Their cousins live in the old shack a couple of blocks down the street from us." Then do you know what happened? They stopped dead in their tracks, shook their heads sadly, and whined, "Too good to be true! We know where he comes from. He's from the other side of the tracks. Oh, he put on a good show; he fooled us for a minute. We thought he was a real whiz—that he could teach the chiropractors a thing or two. But now we know he's too good to be true!"

Too good to be true? What a turnabout! They were silly people back then, weren't they?

Then? Has anything really changed?

Someone says, "Hey, you're intelligent, sensitive, caring. You're perfect for the job but, uh, we don't want women in this business. Tsk! Tsk! Too good to be true!"

Or, "My goodness! You have impeccable credentials. We want responsible people like you living in our building. But, uh, there's a little problem. Tsk! Tsk! You're black! Oh well—too good to be true! Toodle loo!"

51

Or, "Do you know how badly we need someone to teach these kids? You come with the highest recommendations. But, hmmm, you are one of them aren't you? Too good to be true! See you!"

It doesn't take much reflection to realize how our biases change our outlook on the world. First we are impressed with what we see and hear. Then the bias takes over and what we saw and heard we didn't see or hear. Too good to be true! What are the consequences of bias in these situations?

Jesus' townspeople lost out because if they had received Jesus into their lives they would have been enriched by his presence. Jesus lost too! He couldn't be for them what he had intended, and this was his loss. Our biases prevent us from appreciating others' gifts, which then inhibits them from developing these gifts. After all, without others appreciating our talents, we might not be motivated to develop them. "You're too good to be true" is either others' positive assessment of who we are or their dismissal of us altogether! Affirm or deny. The choice is ours.

Somehow!

Mark 4:35-40

He awoke and rebuked the wind and said to the sea:
"Quiet! Be still!" The wind fell off and everything
grew calm. Then he said to them, "Why are you so
terrified? Why are you lacking in faith?"

*L*acking faith? Jesus was a little hard on his friends,
don't you think? I know where my sympathies are. With
his friends. My heart goes out to them because I've been
there—not sailing the ocean blue but flying the friendly
skies! Friendly? Ha! That's a laugh.

Whenever the skies are the least bit unfriendly while
I am flying, I'm not only lacking trust, I am temporarily
transformed into an atheist! The closest I come to being
a Christian is that I don't want to sing "Nearer My God
To Thee" because I'm afraid of getting nearer sooner
than I care to! The only solace I seem to get doesn't
come from trusting a loving savior. Rather, it comes

when the stewardess rolls her cart down the aisle and asks me if I'd like a cocktail.

I have never thought of leaving the flying to Jesus nor have I referred to him as my copilot as some bumper stickers proudly proclaim. Copilot indeed! On the contrary, I make certain that I am sitting in the plane's midsection near the wings so that by vigilantly watching the plane's wing on my side I convince myself that the plane will remain airborne.

I know that there are people on the plane who think of themselves as committed believers. They are the persons who serenely state that when it's time to go, it's time to go. Or they will declare that it's all in God's hands. However, I think that I detect a certain smug satisfaction in their voices suggesting that they know who really trusts and who don't. Oh, I willingly admit that I am not one of those blessed believers who seem to revel in stormy weather to prove how trusting they are. Obviously, they have no problem singing "He's Got The Whole World In His Hands" while I suspect God has gone on vacation and left a madman in charge. See why I sympathize with Jesus' fickle faith friends?

But I've got more on my mind than sympathy for his friends. I'm willing to wager that Jesus' friends had more trust than either Jesus or they thought they had. However, because of the high drama, no one thought to raise a hand and point that out to Jesus. I'd also like to add that the people who seem to be models of trust frequently aren't. Before considering the possibility that Jesus' friends really weren't faithless fellows, I'd like to distinguish bogus trust from the genuine article.

What's a sure sign we're not dealing with the real thing? Anyone who parades his trust is tooting his own horn, not God's. If someone boasts how much he trusts in the Lord and that he's as calm as a cucumber because of that trust, don't fall for it! Trusting is not like developing some muscle in order to impress others. There are no black belt trusters! Maybe boasting about one's trust flatters a person's ego, but boasting is not trusting. Trusting isn't a personal achievement that is rewarded with a trophy for the spiritual mantelpiece.

Nor should we submit to any kind of scolding for not trusting enough—as if we failed because we hadn't put enough effort into trusting. "So you're out of work and you can't find a job. You gotta have a little more faith!" "You're not feeling well? Where's your faith?" "Your marriage is on the rocks? A little more faith in God might help!" The assumption seems to be that it's solely the individual's responsibility for having or not having enough faith in God. Trust enough and you're a success! Don't trust enough and you're a failure. How does genuine trust look?

Think of someone buying an airplane ticket just minutes after completing a stormy flight. There's no guarantee that the next flight will be any less stormy. But the person must visit a dying friend and the next flight is the only way he can get to his friend. Despite great fear, he boards the plane and goes through more hell in the air. On arrival he stammers, "I don't know why or how I got through this. I can't explain. I was frightened to death all the way. But I got here somehow!" This scenario tells us something very important about trust. In spite of the person's anxiety and resistances, he got there—somehow. He would never think of crediting himself for his tenacity. No doubt before he had gotten there, he hoped he would arrive—somehow! Something about this "somehow" symbolizes a power we can rely on without being able to control it. We shrug our shoulders when we speak of "somehow" because we are involved in what has happened but we don't know how—only some-how. Could we say that in that "somehow" the power of God was present?

I think we can see a comparable power at work in Jesus' friends from day one when he invited them to join him. They dropped everything to follow Jesus, including the security of home and career. No doubt they were fearful and apprehensive. Certainly they must have wondered what they had gotten themselves into! Yet in spite of these feelings, they *somehow* did what they didn't think they had it in them to do—namely, they followed Jesus. And they didn't chalk up their decision to follow him as a triumph in trusting! Could we say that here too there was a power at work in this, somehow? And was that power the power of God drawing them forward in faith?

If we think about those moments in our lives when we trusted without reservation, we might not be able to think of many examples. But if we think of the times when we couldn't credit ourselves with being so trusting but somehow muddled through, then these are the times of "somehow trust." We can't claim them as triumphs because they happened somehow! Yet, these are the moments we want to celebrate and identify as moments of faith as we reflect on them.

"Somehow we got through those difficult years of marriage; well, someone or something got us through!" "My knees were shaking but somehow I got up and told them what they were doing was wrong!" Celebrating the moment means we acknowledge that in those "somehow" moments, Christ was present drawing us forward in spite of our resistances. We didn't accomplish a tremendous feat called trusting. It happened. We could describe this equally well by quoting Paul, "I live now, not I, but Christ lives in me,..." and adding, "...somehow!"

Fully Alive —
The Kicker

John 13:31-35

Once Judas had left, Jesus said: "Now is the Son of
Man glorified and God is glorified in him. God will, in
turn, glorify him in himself, and will glorify him
soon."

Jesus tells us that his glory is to glorify his Father
and that his Father's glory is to glorify Jesus. All this
talk about glory reminds me of an expression that
seems to capture what Jesus is saying: It is that the
glory of God is the human person fully alive! But what
does it mean to be fully alive? And in what way is this
the glory of God?

Being fully alive means there is someone or
something that gives us a kick out of life. Someone or
something stimulates us, wakes us up, gets us moving,
stirs the blood, creates excitement! What might that
someone or something be?

Maybe Chevas on the rocks is the kicker!
Or scoring sexually!
Or snorting coke and sniffing glue!
Or waiting for the winning lottery number!
Or getting a buzz on wine!
Or working into the wee hours of the morning!
Or eating chocolates!
Or playing trivial pursuits!

Whatever the kicker, it seems to bring us to life,
doesn't it? We drink the Chevas, and

> get weepy-eyed,
> feel bad about the lot of the poor,
> feel great about how bad we feel about
> everything,
> confess to the persons next to us how much we
> love them.

How nice to feel all this sentiment, all this emotion,
all this love. But then two hours later or the next
morning we are back to normal, except for the
hangover. And nothing has changed, not really! We are
back to square one until the following week when we
re-enact the ritual with Chevas or whatever other
kicker we choose.

The truth is we don't come alive in spite of all the
kicks available. Why? We don't come alive because we
are looking to someone or something outside of
ourselves to give us a kick or a high or a fix—provided
the kick is pain free. We want to feel; oh yes, we do
want to feel! But only what we *want* to feel, and we
don't want pain! If this is the case, then what gives us
the kick also anesthetizes us. It puts us to sleep and
helps us forget. The kick is bogus! It doesn't really bring

us alive; it is a substitute for living. And it is a poor one at that since it screens out awareness of what is happening in us and around us. How, then, do we become fully alive so as to be the glory of God?

I think that we begin to come alive precisely when we recognize that we would prefer to feel nothing, when we would like to be anesthetized. The point of entry where we come alive is that point where we prefer to be deadened. I discovered this for myself a few years ago.

I had occasion to visit a floor in a hospital where all the patients had AIDS. (We all carry sanitized versions in our heads of ministering to others—that too can be our kicker! But what we imagine our ministry will involve and what the reality is are not the same.) I entered one room and there he lay—a man whose body was discolored and inflated with kaposy sarcoma beyond anything I had or have ever seen. Oh, how I wanted to run out of that room! My kick, my stimulus did not include seeing or touching his pain or mine! So I hurried across the hall to another room.

And there I saw a young man who was nothing but skin and bones, Once more, I said to myself that I didn't want or need this; I didn't want to see or know; I just wanted to get out. But the orderly, a young black man, encouraged me to come in and sit down. He wanted me to hear how this young man with AIDS, sitting quietly in a chair, hardly the picture of someone fully alive with God's glory, had helped him in his own grieving over the recent death of his mother. "Oh, he helped me when I was depressed; he listened to me." And as the orderly said this, he looked with affection toward the patient. "Didn't you Jimmy?" And I knew as I listened to the orderly, watched him gently run his fingers through the

young man's hair, and saw him feel his pain, that
here—especially here—in the midst of all this suffering,
the glory of God had to be present. God's glory had to be
here because the orderly was alive to this person's pain,
and this person with precious little time left to live had
been alive to the orderly's pain. For an instant in that
room, I too came alive and knew a little bit more about
the glory of God.

Lord, is this what the glory talk is all about? Is that
what life is about? Your glory was to come alive to the
joy and pain in yourself and in others. You didn't need
any kick, any stimulus, to quicken your life. Surely you
must have been tempted to look away and not feel
where you knew there would be pain. But just as surely
you knew that being fully alive meant getting close to
those areas of life where life must be lived. In doing
that, you truly became the glory of God. May we who
are your followers do the same.

II.

So What's the Problem?

Honoring the Problem's Place in the Sermon

How good is the gospel's good news if it is not the
welcome response to dilemmas or problems that every
day people experience? What disturbs sermon haters is
that frequently preachers offer easy solutions and quick
answers without having adequately explored the
problems. Consequently, the full impact of the good
news is diminished. Preaching solutions honors neither
the way our minds work nor life's complexities, neither
of which admit of easy answers.

Regarding the way we think, isn't it true that we
come alive when we are engaged in a process of
discovery? We delight in figuring things out; working
crossword puzzles; competing to outwit TV game show
contenders; sleuthing over whodunnit mysteries. And
we'd think it silly if someone gave us the answer to the
puzzle before we did our own puzzling. We'd be
indignant if someone informed us whodunnit before we
had done our sleuthing. The excitement is in the
journey. What's as interesting as arriving at our
destination is what we observe along the way and how
we get to where we're going. Eliminate the journeying,

and there's no sense of accomplishment in having arrived.

Consequently, what people need is a preacher who recognizes the importance of leading them on the same journey he has taken from initial questions to tentative conclusions. What they don't need is someone who is fearful of either seriously questioning the text or allowing himself to be questioned by it. If he is fearful, more than likely his sermons will be no more than safe, predictable bromides that create more sermon haters in the congregation.

Identifying an inner struggle or exploring a question that the text provokes may be more liberating than any easy answer the preacher offers. For example, being emotionally abused by a parent or spouse and then being admonished to forgive seven times seventy times is meaningless. What means much more is that there is someone who can express the anger and hurt the person feels toward the one who abused him or her. Identifying the struggle in the sermon is a way of accompanying the pilgrim through fearful, dark places. It is in these places that the preacher needs to be, not resting at the journey's end on some mountain peak.

Wrestling with a biblical text means our struggle is often with Jesus himself. We need not think we are being arrogant or self-centered because we question Jesus' words on some issue like divorce or non-violence. Our questioning springs from the same God-given curiosity we bring to every other human endeavor. Not that we relegate questioning Jesus' words to just one endeavor among many. No, we take this questioning seriously because we understand that his words determine how we will live our lives.

The sermons that follow illustrate how frequently biblical text poses questions and how the questions can be addressed.

How Many
Times?

Matthew 18:21-25

Then Peter came up and asked him, "Lord, when my
brother wrongs me, how often must I forgive him?
Seven times?" "No," Jesus replied, "not seven times;
I say, seventy times seven times."

"*H*ow many times should I forgive? How about
seven?" Peter asked a couple of short questions but they
were loaded—loaded with Peter! He didn't say it but he
might have added, "What do you think of that? Mighty
generous, right? You'd expect me to forgive once. Maybe
twice. Hardly a third time. But you can't beat seven
times, can you?"

Peter was strutting his generosity before Jesus. He
had a forgiving heart and he wanted the boss to know it.
No holds barred here! Others might falter and not have
the strength of character to do what he proposed to do.
They might dwell on their hurts whenever they tried to
forgive, but he could play the hero and let bygones be

bygones. Sure, it wouldn't be easy, but he'd show the others that he could do it. He had willpower!

So he made his proposal. "What do you say, Jesus? How about forgiving seven times?"

Jesus smiles. "C'mon Peter! Seven times. You gotta be kidding. What's seven times? Not seven times! What do you say to seventy times seven?"

Can you imagine Peter's reaction? Seventy times seven? That's 490 times of forgiveness! And Peter had thought seven times was magnanimous. How was Peter going to pull this one off? He tried to imagine forgiving his kid 490 times for mouthing off to him. He wondered where he'd get the energy to forgive his mother-in-law 490 times for telling him he had the biggest mouth of all her sons-in-law. And he shook his head as he mentally rehearsed forgiving his brother 490 times for calling Peter his big dumb brother. How could he manage all this forgiving? But the boss said seventy times seven. No mistaking that. Maybe Jesus knew some secret forgiving formula that would enable Peter to forgive 490 times. If Jesus didn't, Peter would have to swallow hard and tell him he was asking the impossible.

I wonder if Peter took Jesus' answer to his question too literally. I wonder if we, too, take Jesus too literally. Seventy times seven? We know from families with histories of abusive behavior that the victims who say "I forgive" over and over are enabling the abusers to continue their destructive behavior. This kind of forgiveness is an open invitation to abuse. So we need to be careful that in honoring Jesus' remarks on forgiveness we don't perpetuate destructive behavior by repeating over and over "I forgive."

It's possible that Jesus was actually trying to get Peter to see that it wasn't solely nor primarily his responsibility to forgive. Then whose responsibility is it? It is God's. Over and over people either complain that they can't forgive or they sigh that they have already forgiven someone two, three, and four times—but never again.

What is at issue here is what "I" have to do. The focus is on me, I. If I do not do it right, then I feel the burden of guilt. I haven't managed, I haven't succeeded, I failed! I, I, I. Presumably, if I do it right, then I can feel good and get the credit; I've pulled it off! But we forget: it is God who forgives. It is God who has the bigger shoulders and who can bear the burden. Our responsibility is doing what is necessary for forgiveness to happen, not assuming the Herculean task of forgiving. What is this necessary work?

Certainly our task involves owning our anger and being aware how much we'd like to get even and punish the offender. It is important to get all of our feelings out on the table. We need to get in touch with our resentment, shame, jealousy, etc., and not pretend we are beyond these feelings. Once in touch with these feelings, we might also feel guilty because we feel so negative toward the other. Here, too, we need do no more than acknowledge the guilty feeling and let it be.

Further down the road our task is to consider the possibility that the person who has been so offensive and hurtful had at some time in the past been hurt and victimized too. Whatever brought that person to the point of hurting or victimizing us, we do not know. But abusers are frequently people who have been abused.

Once we become aware of this, we might be less judgmental.

Finally, we may begin to see our own complicity in what has happened. We are not the innocent victim we have claimed to be. We too victimize! If not in this situation, at least in others! We tend to see ourselves as the saint and the other as the demon. But we may realize that there is something of the demon in the saint and something of the saint in the demon. We have been victimized and we victimize. This realization helps us understand that what we share in common with the offender is humanity. Each of us is a mixture of dark and light, warts and beauty marks!

In the awareness of our shared humanity, we can begin to discover forgiveness as something that has happened rather than as something that we have to do. God does the forgiving and we are there to witness it. This process by which forgiveness happens is expressed in statements like "I just don't feel I need to do anything. It's not an issue anymore. I can see things from a different perspective now. I don't wish him evil."

Some of us have been hurt so badly that we can't even think about predisposing ourselves to forgive someone. In other words, even the thought of doing the necessary work for forgiveness to occur is out of the question. Admonitions to forgive simply create more guilt and more anxiety. It is at times like this that we need to remind ourselves once more that God has bigger shoulders than we do. God will take care of the matter. God always does.

Consider
the Source

Matthew 5:1-12

When he saw the crowds he went up on the mountainside. After he had sat down his disciples gathered around him, and he began to teach them:

> "How blest are the poor in spirit; the reign of
>   God is theirs.
> Blest too are the sorrowing; they shall be
>   consoled.
> Blest are the lowly; they shall inherit the land.
> Blest are they who hunger and thirst for
>   holiness; they shall have their fill."

*B*y just about everybody's standards being poor, hungry, and oppressed is unfortunate. In other words, it is not good fortune to be living in Soweto Township in South Africa. It is not good fortune to be a little boy with AIDS who has to go to school in a hostile atmosphere. It is not good fortune to be a Raymond Hunthausen, a Charles Curran, or a Terry Waite. It

71

isn't good fortune to be homeless and walking the
streets of New York, Chicago, or Los Angeles, even
during the most pleasant time of the year. No, by just
about everybody's standards, that is not fortunate but
unfortunate. But then, we aren't talking here about just
anybody's standards; we are talking about Jesus'
standards. It is he who said to the poor and the
oppressed and the hungry sitting in front of and
alongside him that they were a fortunate lot. "How blest
are you!" By what logic or by what process of reasoning
could he call them fortunate?

You see, people like myself need some logical
explanation, some reason for Jesus making a statement
that by just about everybody's standards doesn't make
any sense. Moreover, people like myself not only need
an explanation, we are willing to supply an explanation!
We want what Jesus says to make sense. We want
Jesus' remarks about good fortune to fit somebody's
standards as an appropriate, reasonable statement to
give people who find themselves oppressed, poor, and
hungry.

I might satisfy my desire for a logical explanation, for
example, by saying it is fortunate that people are poor.
Only the needy can recognize their dependency on
others and on God. Only then do they see they aren't
self-sufficient, islands set apart. Now there is logic! This
does make sense.

Yet, I can't help feeling uneasy. I do not know how
much of what I say is just so much armchair
philosophizing in which I can make Jesus' strange
remark about being fortunate yield meaning. If I am
honest with myself, my dis-ease might also have to do
with giving an explanation that justifies keeping the

poor of the world poor. After all, look at the "good" that comes out of their being poor!

I may be pressed even further to find an acceptable meaning in Jesus' remark about good fortune by showing how the oppressed are sensitized to the sufferings of others. Their own suffering influences how they see, touch, and hear with remarkable sensitivity the injustices to which their brothers and sisters are subjected. But then I realize that Jesus promised they would rejoice, not that they would develop a greater capacity for more pain. So, Jesus' remark becomes more unintelligible and opaque, not less so.

How then am I to preach comfortably and agreeably on the beatitudes? How am I to make sense out of what Jesus said? Perhaps the answer is I am not supposed to be making any sense at all out of it. For in the last analysis what Jesus said to the poor, the oppressed, and the hungry sitting in front of him and alongside of him made sense not because his words made sense but because *he* made sense to them. It wasn't *what* he said that could ever make sense or fit just about everybody's standards of what made sense. It was that *he* said it. We would say today that he could get away with saying what he did because he was the one whose presence nourished them in their hunger and enriched them even as they remained poor. And it was he who could turn their weeping into laughter even as they continued to cry. What he said about what would happen in the future made sense to them only because *he* made sense to them the way he touched them in the present moment.

What all of this suggests to me is that we may never be able to make sense out of Jesus' remark about how fortunate all these unfortunate people are unless we touch and are touched by the poor, the oppressed, and the hungry sitting in front of us and beside us. So, when Archbishop Tutu told his brothers and sisters sitting in front of and beside him that God really loved them but that many of them would have to die before there was liberation, his words "made sense" only because *he* made sense to them, only because the future for which they longed was somehow already embodied in his present concern for them.

Does this mean that we dare not preach the beatitudes unless we are or have been where we tell others how fortunate they are to be? It is a question worth pondering, isn't it? How fortunate we are!

Voice
of God

Genesis 22:1-18

But the LORD's messenger called to him from heaven,
"Abraham, Abraham!" "Yes, Lord," he answered. "Do
not lay your hand on the boy," said the messenger.
"Do not do the least thing to him. I know now how
devoted you are to God, since you did not withhold
from me your own beloved son."

*W*hat does God want of me? Or, what am I supposed
to do in my life? These are variations of the same
question. They are spelled out more concretely in other
questions. Should I marry? Should I stay single? Get
divorced? Go to college? Have children? How many? In
seeking answers we wonder if we are doing what God
wants us to do. At one time we think that God wants us
to do one thing; at another time we do something
completely different and wonder if this is what God had
in mind.

What does God want? What shall I do? The matter is
complicated when I consider that what I think God

wants me to do or what I think I want to do may be
more what others think I ought to do. The voices are
many: get married, settle down, be a teacher, be an
actor. The advice we get about what God wants or what
we ought to do becomes very specific as when we are
told that God wants husbands, wives, children to be
husbands, wives, children in clearly defined ways.

Tensions, anxieties, and worries abound when after
several years of doing what we think we are supposed to
be doing, we begin to suspect that maybe God really
wants something else of us. Then we anguish over past
decisions and paths taken that we suspect we ought not
to have made and now feel we must abandon. What
shall we do? Have we wasted our lives? Or are we about
to make new decisions that will end up being as wrong
as the ones we have made?

I think if we consider the Abraham-Isaac story, we
may gain some perspective on the struggle I have
described. We can read this story as the story of God
who changes his mind about what he wants Abraham to
do, or we can read it as the story of Abraham who has a
change of mind as to what God has in mind for him and
Isaac.

If it is a story about God who changes his mind, then
we have a God who tests Abraham's fidelity by asking
him to sacrifice Isaac and subsequently commanding
him not to. Whether or not God would fool around with
someone's mind as he did with Abraham's, I choose not
to consider.

I think the story makes more sense if we read it as a
story about a man who tries to remain faithful to his
own understanding of what God wants and then

discovers that he, Abraham, has to change his mind regarding God's will.

From Abraham's perspective, God can't seem to make up his mind. All Abraham can do is remain faithful to his perception of what God wants. But if we were to look at this from God's perspective, then Abraham simply failed to get a clear understanding of what God wanted. Abraham's fidelity to doing God's will eventually led him to understand what God had always wanted of Abraham—that he not sacrifice his son.

Could it be that we too have experiences similar to Abraham's? At one time we think that God wants one thing, at another time something else. Then we wonder, "What am I supposed to do? I've been brought up to think that God wants me to do what my mother/father/church/country/friends tell me God wants. But then I feel that I have to say 'no' to them somewhere along the line because now I understand what God really wants." It is no wonder that we experience anxiety and guilt in coming to a different understanding of what we are to do with our lives. For a long period of time, our loyalties have been to previous understandings of who God is, what God wants, what we ought to be doing in life. And now we feel on one level that we are unfaithful to our commitments. Yet on another level we sense God is asking something else of us. It isn't clear what God wants and we are anxious. What shall we do?

The important thing is fidelity—commitment to the struggle to determine what God wants of us. Paradoxically, we have to suffer our feeling of being unfaithful to God on one level so that we can remain faithful to God's call on another. It would be nice if there were no uncertainty or ambiguity or darkness in deciding what we are to do. But I do not think this is possible.

Since remaining faithful means a readiness to change direction or course of action and therefore a willingness to acknowledge that what God wants means a reversal of how we have understood God's will in our lives, we must necessarily experience anxiety. We need to be faithful to what we have come to believe is what we ought to do, even if it means a 360-degree turn as it did for Abraham.

Who Needs
Whom?

John 15:1-8

"Live on in me, as I do in you. No more than a branch
can bear fruit of itself apart from the vine, can you
bear fruit apart from me. I am the vine, you are the
branches. He who lives in me and I in him, will
produce abundantly, for apart from me you can do
nothing."

"I am the vine, you are the branches." The message
seems direct and unambiguous. Without me, Jesus says,
you will perish. Just as branches lopped off the vine dry
up and die, so, too, anyone not "in Christ" will die. But I
am not certain the message is all that simple.

Perhaps we can understand what the message is if we
consider what Jesus seems to be reacting against when
he uses the image of the vine and the branch. I think he
is reacting to me-ism. Me-ism regards independence as
the most important value in life: I am the center of
everything. Me-ism comes disguised as racism (my
race), as nationalism (my nation), as ageism (my age),

79

as sexism (my sex). Me and mine are all important. When we emphasize our independence, our self-sufficiency, we end up in a world in which we are cut off and separated from others. Jesus tells us through this imagery that we are not independent, and if we think we are, we shall die. What else is he telling us?

That we all depend on him? That we are nothing without him? Yes, something like that, but only something. The idea that we ought to be utterly dependent and that we are nothing unless we are so dependent is what I call you-ism: I can't do anything; I depend on you; I am helpless. A lot of people have been trained in dependency to such an extent that their sole source of gratification as well as their self-esteem is derived through another. These people even depend upon God in an unhealthy way, "Why doesn't God do this? Or that? Why doesn't he take care of me?" We can't see ourselves as co-creators if we assume this utterly dependent role. Given the context of this homily, I would call these needy, dependent persons, people who have the clinging vine syndrome! There is no room to breathe in relationships in which people are so dependent on others or one another that they can't function apart from others. This is unhealthy! If Jesus doesn't preach me-ism or you-ism, what does he preach?

Could it be that Jesus is not speaking about independence or dependence but interdependence? What I call we-ism. While it is true that the branches would be nothing without the vine, it is also true that the vine wouldn't look like much without the branches. Interdependence means mutuality and reciprocity. You can say "mother" only when there is a child. "Doctor"

means there is a patient; "teacher" means there is a
student; "preacher" means there are listeners. You can't
have one without the other. When it comes to our
experience of the vine and the branches, we can ask
this: how can Jesus be our savior or liberator unless we
acknowledge the need to be saved and liberated? Recall
the incident in Jesus' life where he was not able to heal
people because they didn't believe he could heal them.
All the good will in the world is of no avail if we never
avail ourselves of it. All of us, including Jesus, are
interdependent.

The image of the vine and the branches is neither
about me-ism nor you-ism; it is about collaboration:
we-ism.

Winning Our Way
into the Heart of God

Mark 7:14-23

"Are you, too, incapable of understanding?" he asked
them. "Do you not see that nothing that enters a man
from outside can make him impure? It does not pen-
etrate his being, but enters his stomach only and
passes into the latrine." Thus did he render all foods
clean.

Probably everyone here has either gone on a diet or
will go on one. Why do we diet? The obvious reason is to
lose weight. Who wants to lug around an extra
twenty-five or fifty pounds? It isn't healthy!

Another reason why we diet is that we want to appear
acceptable to others and to ourselves. We want approval
and we hope to gain acceptance through controlling the
kind of food we eat. In our desire to be acceptable, we
are not unlike the crowds to whom Jesus preached.

They too sought approval and acceptance. Being
religious people they were especially concerned about
God's acceptance of them. We might think it strange

that one of the ways they hoped to be acceptable to God was through the kinds of food they ate. Some foods were considered pure, and some, impure. By abstaining from impure foods and eating only what was pure, they sought to be acceptable. We who diet do not call foods pure or impure, but for all practical purposes, we might as well. We regard food high in calories as forbidden and food low in calories as clean or good. We avoid cakes, pies, cookies, ice cream, and fried foods, and we buy fruits, vegetables, diet sodas, and lean meats. Although we disclaim any religious motivation in dieting, we pursue our dieting with a fervor that is religious.

And does all this dieting make us any more acceptable to ourselves or to others? I don't think so. We can make ourselves no more acceptable to others and ourselves through the food we eat than Jesus' audience could make themselves acceptable through the food they did or didn't eat. Before I explain why acceptance is not something we can win or not win through food, I would like to address those who don't need to go on diets. If you think you are free from the problem I have described, you are wrong. While dieting is one way of striving for acceptance, it is not the only way.

Any attempt on our part to say or do the right thing in the right place at the right time in order to be acceptable to others or to ourselves is a variation on the theme I have been discussing. An acquaintance of mine told me that after his divorce he experienced a tremendous need to be accepted. He felt so unloved that he entered into a relationship as soon as possible. He then tried very hard to please her by anticipating her needs and being sensitive to her feelings. He wanted to say and do exactly the right thing because he needed her approval so desperately. Why would his efforts be doomed to failure?

The answer to this question is the same answer I would give to those of us who diet and hope to win approval through dieting. We cannot set conditions for acceptance. "If I do this, then that will happen" is magical thinking. Through our conditions we want to control the way a relationship should or should not develop. Push the right buttons and *Abracadabra!* the other will accept us and we will be acceptable to ourselves! Jesus knew this wouldn't work in relation to God, and it won't work in our relationships with God, with others, and with ourselves. What works?

Jesus' mission was to announce the good news that we are already acceptable in God's eyes. We can't earn it; we don't deserve it. It is there even before we ask for it. Jesus' baptismal experience was God's revelation to him that he was God's beloved, and Jesus preached that everybody is God's beloved, without qualification. Paul Tillich, the great theologian, spoke of our needing the courage to accept God's acceptance. This is a challenge because we are so conditioned to think acceptance is conditional that we refuse to believe it could be otherwise. But God's acceptance comes without strings attached. We don't need to win our way into the heart of God. We've always been there and we always will be.

Doubts That Damn and Doubts That Save

John 20:19-31

It happened that one of the Twelve, Thomas (the name means "Twin"), was absent when Jesus came. The other disciples kept telling him: "We have seen the Lord!" His answer was, "I will never believe it without probing the nail prints in his hands, without putting my finger in the nail marks and my hand into his side."

*T*homas has been given a bad rap for doubting, and it is about time we reconsider our judgment. It is possible that Thomas' doubting was not the action of someone living in the dark but of someone who valued his own light as a means of discovering the truth. People who live their lives in darkness frequently are doubters, but not Thomas' kind. Who are these doubters? And in what sense can we say their doubts damn?

Many children grow up never trusting or believing that what they do in life is of any value or significance. For example, a little boy runs home from school one day and shows his mother a drawing he made at school. He is beaming, proud of what he has done. Yet when his mother looks at the drawing, she is either not interested or she points out how the boy could have done better. Dejected, the boy walks away feeling that what he has done is worthless.

Or perhaps a young girl brings home a report card and on the card there are seven Bs and one C. Dad looks at the card and chooses to focus on the one C. Why is it, he wonders, that she has this one C? Hasn't she studied enough? He doesn't take the time to tell her what a great job she has done by getting all the Bs. Disappointed, the girl leaves the room. Is it any wonder that in such an atmosphere children don't develop any sense of competence in their own abilities? They do not learn to trust that what they do is of value or worth because they receive no confirmation from their parents. Not only are they unconfirmed that they are shining lights, they are also crippled by self-doubt. This is the doubt that damns and puts them in the dark.

Why is the doubt so damning? Adults can distinguish the difference between their judgments being questioned and themselves being questioned, but children cannot make that nice distinction. In other words, constantly pointing out what another hasn't done properly erodes both a person's capacity to do something worthwhile and to be a person of value. Children learn to doubt themselves. They can't make moves in one direction or the other because no matter which way they move, they are wrong. They then remain stuck; they are dammed up; nothing can flow. People dammed up in this way are very insecure. They cannot answer questions with any confidence. "Did you

86

like the movie?" "Well, I don't know." "Do you have any
feelings about so and so?" "Well..." Such people cannot
believe in God in any mature way because they don't
believe in their own ability to believe in any meaningful
way. They accept what others have to say because they
don't trust their own judgment. Living with this
damning doubt is indeed living in the dark.

There is another kind of doubting, however, which
presupposes we no longer live in darkness. When we
treasure our ability to question and have had others
affirm us in our questioning, then our doubting can be a
sign of health, not sickness. Healthy doubting means we
are able to call into question our attitudes, ideas,
opinions, and theories and not think the world is coming
to an end because of our questioning. If, as children, we
imagine God as a kind old gentleman who will always
protect everybody, and one day someone close to us dies,
then we may doubt our belief in God as the one who
protects against all injury. In this sense, doubting is an
intelligent way of registering a lack of correspondence
between what we think God is and what God really is.

To use another example, perhaps we think of God as
white and male. At some point we say to ourselves, "Is
that really the case? Is God really white and male?
Maybe God is as much mother as father, or black as
white, or none of these at all!" For a while we may be in
the dark. We thought we had figured out who God was,
but then we come to realize this is not the case at all.
God—like friends—surprises us, and we can be
surprised because we come to doubt certainties and
ways of thinking about God.

As we have already noted, this kind of doubting can
be healthy because it means we are maturing in our

way of thinking and relating to others, the world, and God. It can also be painful because it means we have to surrender ways of relating and thinking without necessarily arriving at any deeper understanding to replace old ways. Here we need to trust that even if we aren't sure where we are going, there is One who is guiding us. "Blessed are those who do not see and have believed," but do so because they see that they do not see—not because they have been coerced into believing.

III.

Preaching Jesus

Proclaiming an Imperfectly Human Jesus

It is my business to listen to novice preachers deliver sermons. And if anyone merits being president of the Sermon Haters Club, I do. Few can claim to have been overpowered by as many sermons on Jesus the mighty god-man as I have. I refer to sermonic variations on the god-man theme as well—for example, the divine child, the pre-existent Word, the Second Person of the Trinity, and so on. Less overpowering but still formidable is the preached Jesus who is perfectly caring, perfectly understanding, perfectly patient, perfectly suffering, etc. Everything this Jesus does, he does perfectly!

Since I am overpowered by the Jesus of these sermons, I have often wondered if Jesus appeared to his contemporaries as the great god-man who overpowered them too! Were they rendered speechless as the King of Kings and Lord of Lords strolled down their streets? Was Jesus so obviously the god-man? Or is it possible that his contemporaries were unaware of anything remarkable about Jesus for some time? And once the light dawned, did they observe something so compelling that they could think of nothing else?

The problem with so many sermons about the god-man or the perfectly human Jesus is that *this man* is lost in the process. Jesus was a caring, sensitive, understanding person, but he could also ignore his relatives, be testy with his followers, and rail against his enemies. He worked miracles, but he was powerless to help people who didn't want his assistance. He loved to be alone, but he also loved to party. While he associated with respectable members of Jewish society, he also hobnobbed with the Jewish mafia, the tax collectors. He had a predilection for dining with people to whom most of us wouldn't offer a sandwich at the back door.

The sermons I prefer hearing are sermons about this man, not The God-Man. I'm not interested in being blinded by the brilliance of his majesty or divinity. Nor do I care to hear about someone who is the perfect embodiment of love, kindness, and humility. Am I denying Jesus' true identity by preferring not to listen to sermons stressing his divinity? No. What I desire is to listen to someone preach a Jesus so thoroughly human that I discover the "more than human" here. Give me someone that preaches a Jesus who was labeled a drifter, a loser, and a loony as well as forgiving, patient, and wise. Then I will cry for joy, "He's one of us! He's where I am!" Give me more time to reflect on what I've heard and I might add, "He's one of us, but he's also more than that! Jesus is Lord!" I would rather be gently led into confessing Jesus is Lord than overpowered by the rhetoric of divine razzle-dazzle. I hope that the sermons that follow suggest the kind of Jesus I prefer to hear preached.

God's Pride
and Joy

Luke 4:1-13

Jesus, full of the Holy Spirit, then returned from the
Jordan and was conducted by the Spirit into the
desert for forty days, where he was tempted by the
devil.

*A*fter Jesus was baptized he was sent into the desert
where he engaged the dark power in battle. Don't you
think Jesus wondered how this could happen to him
after what he had experienced in his baptism? Don't you
think he was downright disappointed with the change
in the neighborhood? Not to mention the neighbor?
When he was being baptized, he bathed in the
awareness that he was God's pride and joy. "You are my
beloved Son. With you I am well pleased." Those were
the words that filled his ears and lifted his spirits. He
felt so special! We know something of that feeling, don't
we?

We've known what it's like to be riding high!

We've been to the mountaintop and felt terrific!
We've had visions of a promising future!
We've had our own great expectations!
If we know these feelings, then we can understand
why Jesus would feel so let down at finding himself in a
god-forsaken desert.

Don't you agree that going into the desert after being
on such a high is really traveling in a strange direction?
Don't you think Jesus wondered why he, God's pride
and joy, would now be facing a hostile power? We know
something of his feeling, don't we?

We've found ourselves going nowhere when we had
believed we had been going somewhere.

We've found ourselves confronting some mean demons
when we believed and hoped we had a promising future.

We've been disappointed when our rising star turned
into a falling meteor—down, down, down!

But it was in the desert that he was tested. It was
here that he had to sort out what being God's pride and
joy meant and what it didn't mean. We know the
feeling, don't we? Because we too have our desert spaces
where we've got to find out what it means to be who we
are. We have to get things cleared up!

"You're God's pride and joy because you're a
superstar! So do your thing! Change these stones into
bread!" That's what the dark power proposed to Jesus.
Do something spectacular! Perform! We know what he
wants. We know it well:

Get A's and shine!
Make it big in Little League!
Say and do the right thing so you can get ahead!
Smile when you're told to smile!
Cry when you're told to cry!

Just perform! You gotta do something to be the loved one, to be the pride and joy.

But no. Jesus doesn't buy this razzle-dazzle. All this show and no substance! This temptation to be an everlasting crowd-pleaser! It doesn't work!

So the dark power tries another tack. "I'll give you city hall! There's power there. They'll take care of you! Just cozy up to them! Let them know you can work within the system." Imagine all the power! What could Jesus do with all that power? Get everybody rushing to his side. No negotiations here! No sitting down and talking with the enemy. No way! Power means force, getting things done quickly. We understand power. Power is:

> gunning the motor,
> making a fist,
> threatening, intimidating, yelling louder,
> flexing muscles,
> showing the powerless the spectacle of guns
> and ammo,
> being in control.

Power is being special! Power is glorious!

But no, he doesn't want to be a power broker. Power can't be *it*, the be-all and end-all of life.

A third time Jesus is confronted. The dark power carries him to the parapet of the Temple and challenges him, "If you're God's pride and joy, then jump off this parapet! He'll see to it that nothing happens to you." How appealing! We know the temptation. Wouldn't someone who really loved us take care of us and cushion our fall so we wouldn't:

get cancer,
or heart disease,
or be run over by a car,
or be betrayed by friends, lovers, spouses,
children.

God would be there to catch us. Isn't that what it means to be special?

But Jesus won't accept the dark power's challenge because his understanding of being God's pride and joy differs. You don't test someone you love by demanding proof of that love. You don't play games!

So through this confrontation with the dark power, Jesus gets a clearer picture about what being God's pride and joy is not. It is not performing, wielding power, or being free from suffering. Why, then, is he special?

He is special not because of anything that he does but because he is who he is. He has no need to justify himself or prove anything. Coming from the hands of God is reason enough for being God's pride and joy. And I think that Jesus' desert experience prepared him to preach a similar message to everyone he met. We too are special, not because of what we have accomplished but because we come from the hands of God. There is always the temptation to prove we are worthy of being special rather than acknowledging that there is nothing we have done to deserve the designation "special" or "God's pride and joy."

Today we ask the Father to help us realize in a new way the status we enjoy as God's pride and joy.

Narrow
Door

Luke 13:22-30

Someone asked him, "Lord, are they few in number
who are to be saved?" He replied: "Try to come in
through the narrow door. Many, I tell you, will try to
enter and be unable. When once the master of the
house has risen to lock the door and you stand outside
knocking and saying, 'Sir, open for us,' he will say in
reply, 'I do not know where you come from.'"

I am amazed. Someone asked Jesus a simple question
and he practically bit the fellow's head off! How unlike
Jesus! How out of character! What set him off? Why so
touchy? What had he eaten? Did he have indigestion? A
bad headache? Wasn't there any Pepto-Bismol around?
DiGel? Tylenol—Extra Strength?

Do you think his tart reply had something to do with
the one who asked the question? What was there about
the fellow that struck the wrong chord? I bet this person
wasn't just anyone but someone special, someone you
wouldn't want to turn away from your door—someone

97

important, from city hall, maybe, or the chancery with
the right connections and credentials. Not just any Tom,
Dick, or Harry!

Yeh, this person must have been concerned about who
was and who wasn't getting in—checking to make
certain the right people were getting in.

So why was Jesus so upset—furious, really—when
this somebody who wasn't just anybody and certainly
not a nobody put this question to him: "Master, only a
handful can make it, right? Only those with reserved
seats will be admitted, right? No johnnie-come-latelies,
right? There will be limitations, restrictions,
specifications regarding color, ethnic background,
socio-economic status, right?

"Undoubtedly there will be signs on the front lawn of
the heavenly palace indicating in a pleasant and
congenial way that only the right people can enter, that
is, kind of white, mostly white really, all white actually.
Right?

"And standing guard with arms folded at the front
door of the palace there will be elders, elegantly robed
in white, kindly informing any women who'd entertain
the thought of crashing the old boys' club that they can't
get in because...because they aren't the right sex. But as
compensation and as a sign the old boys harbor no ill
feelings, the lovely ladies could Spic 'N Span the brass
railings leading up to the palace's narrow door. Then
the ladies could do what they do best!"

Yes, it's not so hard to understand why Jesus got so
upset with the questioner and his question. It's not so
hard to understand why Jesus rolled up his sleeves,
pointed directly at that someone who wasn't just

anyone, who had the right connections, who could drop the right names, and said,

"I dare *you* to try and get in. I just dare you. It'll be a tight squeeze; a hard fit; you'll get stuck in the door; you'll block the free flow of traffic. You'll push and shove, you'll wheeze and squeeze, *but* you won't make it! And you'll be upset and fret and plead and cry, 'Hey I deserve to get in! I'm special! I hang around with the right kind of people. I read the right periodicals. I go to the right breakfast prayer services. I know the right dogmas.'

"But guess what? I've got news for you! The laugh is on you! *I* don't know the right people! Surprise! *I* don't know anything about the old boys' club except that they never let me in either! *I* don't know the right cliques with their whites only, men only, admittance policies. *I* don't know the right words to say to the right people in power. *Right* is not a word as important in my vocabulary as it is in yours!"

But the story doesn't end there. After Jesus has made his point he goes on to say, "And people will come from the east and the west and from the north and the south and will recline at table in the kingdom of God." In other words the kingdom door is as wide and spacious as the ocean for those who don't claim to be the right people, who don't claim power or fame or position to make them right. The door is wide open for those who don't feel they belong to the right group—for those who don't claim to be an exclusive club.

And the reason the kingdom door is so wide for them is that they are special in God's eyes and that is all that counts. These are the children of God who will have a heavenly blast because they have been made right by

God. They are special not for what they do, but because God has made them special in his sight!

Necessary Obstacles

Mark 8:27-33

He began to teach them that the Son of Man had to suffer much, be rejected by the elders, the chief priests, and the scribes, be put to death, and rise three days later. He said these things quite openly. Peter then took him aside and began to remonstrate with him. At this he turned around and, eyeing the disciples, reprimanded Peter: "Get out of my sight, you satan! You are not judging by God's standards but by man's!"

*P*eter and Jesus had a disagreement that day, a misunderstanding. More than that, they exchanged strong words. Only seconds before their relationship had seemed to be on such sure footing. Jesus had asked his disciples the question, "Who do you think I am?" Peter was the first to respond. "You are the Messiah!" Jesus must have been delighted with Peter's answer. But then the unexpected happened. Jesus went on to say that the road ahead would not be smooth, that there would be suffering ahead, even death for him. But Peter didn't buy this, and he began arguing with Jesus—told him he shouldn't talk that way! Jesus got angry and let Peter have it—told him that he was trying to make him trip and fall!

We can imagine the isolation, the loneliness that each man must have felt. When you are close to someone and you have a falling out, isn't that unfortunate? Isn't it unnecessary? Isn't it an obstacle to communication that could have been avoided?

We think of a misunderstanding in a relationship as a flaw, a weakness, an interruption. Think of your own relationships with friends, parents, children, spouse, or God. You think you know them, then *Wham!*, one day you have a misunderstanding. There are strong words, anger, even tears. You feel isolated and you wonder what went wrong. How could anything so good turn so bad so quickly?

But I have a question. Is it really all that bad? How could Peter have known better unless there was a misunderstanding? Were it not for these misunderstandings, could the relationship between Jesus and Peter have developed at all? In the isolation of the moment, each friend had time to reflect on the other's assumptions about him. Only in that moment could Peter realize how much he didn't know this man he had been following, and in that moment Jesus came to a deeper understanding of Peter's limits and expectations regarding him. The lonely moment, not the moments of togetherness, is the precious moment to reflect on the direction in which a relationship is going.

It is through the misunderstanding and not in spite of it that Jesus and Peter deepen their relationship.

Misunderstanding contains the seed of new understanding.

Jesus' experiences are instructive for us. Through his relationship with Peter, we realize that relationships flourish not simply because of mutual understanding but also because of misunderstandings. In those moments of misunderstanding when we come to see that we have assumed what we ought not to have assumed, we may be in a position to see the other and ourselves in a new way. We come to a deeper understanding of one another. Friendships, love affairs, and marital relationships can't be nourished simply on the basis of togetherness and harmony. Paradoxically, we come to know one another not simply by knowing "where we stand" with one another but also by "not knowing where we stand." Jesus' and Peter's misunderstanding is the gift they bring us today.

Family
Man

Mark 3:20-35

He returned to the house with them and again the crowd assembled, making it impossible for them to get any food whatever. When his family heard of this they came to take charge of him, saying, "He is out of his mind"; while the scribes who arrived from Jerusalem asserted, "He is possessed by Beelzebul," and "He expels demons with the help of the prince of demons."

*T*here is a line from the gospel that we easily could miss if we didn't listen carefully. It's a line we preachers would prefer explaining by explaining it away. We'd like to say it doesn't say what it does say. We'd rather cough or sneeze or mumble this line than proclaim it as clearly as any other line in the gospel. Why? Because the line raises eyebrows and causes people to whisper, "Really? Well, I never would have thought that Jesus..., of all people!"

Family Man

Frankly, I think Mark would have preferred omitting
the line from the gospel. But I'm delighted that he
didn't. Because it sheds new light on Jesus' family,
brings a sigh of relief to families who have their own
problems, and challenges us to rethink Jesus.

Do you know which line I mean? I'll tell you but you'll
have to wait for a minute. I'm going to take my time and
not blurt it out! I don't want to be accused of disturbing
your faith. So let me invite you to place yourselves in
the following scene for a couple of minutes.

Let's suppose you're a young couple with a baby boy,
your only child, who is only a few months old. You've
come to church on a fine summer day. As you enter, a
kindly looking old gentleman whom you have frequently
seen but never met approaches you. He asks you if he
could speak to you for a minute. You smile and say,
"Why, of course!"

The old man pats the little boy's head, tickles his chin,
and tells you that the infant in your arms is going to be
a real troublemaker! What would you say? "Hey, that's
great news! Just what we wanted to hear!" or "Gee,
that's not what we had in mind for our son," or "Are you
crazy?" Maybe you'd just smile and keep a respectful
silence. That suits the old man because he's in a chatty
mood as he continues laying out the future for your son.

Let's suppose he tells you that when your son is
twelve years old, the three of you will take a trip to the
Windy City for a few days. While there, your son will go
off on his own without your permission. Then the old
man will chuckle and tell you that you will have an
anxiety attack and go through a ton of Maalox before
finding the lad conversing with a few priests inside a
church on Clark Street. And the only explanation your

son will offer for his behavior is "I have more important things to do than hang around with you folks!"

Would you be brimming with gratitude toward the old man? Would you finally tell him to keep his good news to himself? But let's suppose you couldn't even raise a word of protest like "Stop" or "Wait" or "C'mon" or "Poppycock" because the old man was really on a roll and nothing but nothing could stop him. Suppose he would go on to tell you that when your son reached his thirties he would occasionally ignore you and your relatives when you wanted to visit him. Would you feel the old man had insulted you? Would you tell your spouse that you never wanted to run into this old loony again?

And as you began making a hasty departure out the church doors, let's suppose the old man shuffled out behind you. Quickening your pace, you hear him mumble something about your son preaching—telling others to take a strong stand against parents who tried to prevent them from following your son's example.

Then let's suppose the old man gets a parting shot and shouts energetically that one fine summer day several years hence you would be so frustrated with your son that you would attempt to commit him to a psychiatric ward! Then he would laugh, do a jig, and comfort you with the news that a hundred years later everybody would look back to your family with admiration. They would think of your family as a model for all families, and they'd set aside a special day to celebrate your family. And they'd call your family "The Holy Family!"

Crazy, huh? But as you have probably guessed, the family I've been talking about is The Holy Family. It doesn't seem right, does it? When we think of the holy family, we think of peace, harmony, and togetherness. We have a holy card image of Jesus, Mary, and Joseph, which doesn't match the reality of this real family.

The truth is, everything I have said is in accord with what we read in the gospels. When Mary and Joseph brought Jesus to the Temple, Simeon, a Temple elder, informed them that Jesus was destined for the rise and fall of many people. Remember the line I told you is an eye opener? It is Mark 3:21. Jesus' family wanted to lock him up; they wanted to put him away. Why? Because they thought he was out of his mind. They thought he was nuts! But why was his family convinced Jesus was crazy?

Because he didn't behave the way they thought he should. He was saying things that disturbed them. For example in Matthew (10:34-38) he says he hasn't come to make things comfy for families, that those who love their parents more than him aren't worthy of him. I advise you to read the whole passage. It is sobering news for people who think of Jesus only as the Prince of Peace!

What are we to think about all this? That Jesus had no respect for his family? No. That they never got along with one another? Hardly. We know that his mother was with him to the end. She stood at the foot of the cross. What I'd like to suggest is that there is clear evidence of tension between Jesus and his family. That tension is dramatically illustrated today.

One lesson we can learn from the gospel is clear. If we think the best family or the most successful family ought to be free of strife or disagreement, then Jesus' family would never have made the best family list.

Certainly, if we think holiness means concord, peace, and harmony, freedom from any disagreement or hostility, then Jesus' family wouldn't come close to being called holy. There is little accomplished by pretending there are no disagreements, or by hiding them under the rug, or by demanding that they go away. And why should any of us hide disagreements or deny tensions within our families? The good news is that neither disagreements nor tensions disqualify us from becoming what we are challenged to be—holy families!

Downward
Mobility

Acts 1:1-11

They were still gazing up into the heavens when two
men dressed in white stood beside them. "Men of
Galilee," they said, "why do you stand here looking
up at the skies? This Jesus who has been taken from
you will return, just as you saw him go up into the
heavens."

*W*ho doesn't know the meaning of upward mobility?
Who hasn't aspired to being upwardly mobile? At least a
little bit? Honestly, I think we live and move and have
our being yearning for upward mobility. So that there's
no mistake about what we mean when we refer to
upward mobility, it means:

> if we are drinking Elmer's Scotch, we aspire to
> drink Chevas;
> if we live in a two bedroom flat on Podunk
> Street, we've got our eyes on a suburban
> five-bedroom home;

if we are driving around in a form-fitting Pinto,
we're figuring the cost of a Continental.

It means wanting to move up from being the clerk to
owning the store,

moving from being a ground-floor receptionist
to being the secretary for a top exec on the
thirtieth floor,
getting real diamonds, not imitation,
sending the kids to an Ivy League school, not
the local college.

The feast of the Ascension is the feast of upward
mobility par excellence! Up, up and away! Jesus moves
upward. His disciples must have thought "upward
mobility" when they watched Jesus leave the scene.
They probably figured he had gone through enough; he
deserved to move up and sit on the power throne next to
the Big Boss and be the righthand man. After all,
everybody knows that if you move up in life, you ought
to have power.

But while they were looking up, longing to be there
some day themselves, a couple of angels tapped them on
the shoulders and asked them why they were looking at
the sky. The boss's son was going away for a little while,
but he'd be back.

Coming back? Jesus' friends must have scratched
their heads. Coming back? For what?

Whoever heard of downward mobility?

Who would move back to the core after living in the
suburbs?

Who would exchange Perrier for tap water?

Who would give up the filet and eat hot dogs?

Who would go back to a form-fitting Pinto?

Who would give up more for less? Bigger for smaller? Power for weakness? Weakness?

It doesn't make sense! When everybody wants to go up, why does he want to come down?

Maybe because life isn't lived up there. When you're on an upper, riding high, you've got to come down. Maybe going up is a way of disconnecting, forgetting, distancing. "Now that we're here, let's just forget about where we've been and who we've left behind!" The danger of the upward reach is that we don't look back. We lose touch with the earth and the concerns of the earth: poverty, injustice, ecology. Our ascensions bring us into the clouds where our "spiritual" concerns are about God and me, Jesus as my personal Lord and Savior.

But Jesus is not to be found in that suburban haven in the sky. He is downwardly mobile. Moving down and in is the way of entering, of being in touch, of getting connected with where people live their lives. The downwardly mobile is of the earth and earthy—that is, involved in the messy business of day-to-day living: broken relationships, homelessness, dying children, etc.

Jesus' departure was not a one-way ticket. And his message to all the brothers and sisters is the same that the angels delivered to his friends when they looked upward away from the earth. "Why are you standing there looking at the sky?" Upward mobility is not Jesus' message; downward mobility is. "Don't leave behind the broken-hearted; don't forget your suffering brothers and sisters because if you want to find me, that's where I will be."

Blessed
Assurance

John 21:15-19

A third time Jesus asked him, "Simon, son of John, do you love me?" Peter was hurt because he had asked a third time, "Do you love me?" So he said to him: "Lord, you know everything. You know well that I love you." Jesus told him, "Feed my sheep."

"Do you love me?"
"Yes."
"Do you love me?"
"Yes."
"Do you love me?"
"Yes."
Did Jesus have a hearing problem when he asked Peter three times if Peter loved him? Or was he playing some kind of game? Maybe Jesus was settling the score with Peter for having three times denied knowing him.

Perhaps we'll find the answer to this question if we reflect on an experience in which we had been deeply hurt by a betrayal. Think of a friend or lover or spouse whom you loved and trusted. Think, too, of the many times you shared your hopes, dreams, and secrets with that person. Think how you assumed that if anyone understood you it was this person. You assumed that the two of you would go to bat for each other anywhere at anytime. You assumed!

But then the person betrayed you. The shared secrets were no longer secret. Even your enemies now knew them. Or one day someone informed you that your lover or spouse had been cheating on you—for months! You felt hurt, resentful, and vulnerable. You didn't know if you would recover.

Then let's suppose something unexpected happens. Several months later, your friend or lover or spouse shows up on your front steps wanting to make amends. Wanting to be forgiven for what he or she has done. What do you say? How do you react? Maybe you simply want to sit down and talk things over. And if you do, during the course of your conversation you might ask, "Do you really love me?" Considering what you had gone through, you certainly would want some reassurance about the future of the relationship. Suppose the person said, "Yes, I really love you." Would that assurance be enough? Would you say, "Great! Let's put the whole matter behind us and get on with life!" I doubt it.

You might find yourself still wondering whether this person loves you. And why not? He or she made promises before and broke them. What's to prevent him or her from breaking them again? You have real doubts. So no wonder you ask a second time, "Do you love me?" And suppose a second time he or she says, "Yes, I love you." Would that finally satisfy you? Now could you turn your attention to other matters? Like chatting about the weather? Or discussing a novel you've read? I doubt it. What then? Raise the same question you have already raised twice? And what possible reason would you have for doing this?

Because this time what is at issue is your own worth. By this I mean a betrayal leaves the betrayed agonizing over what he or she had done to merit betrayal. Was it your looks? The way you spoke? Or dressed? Or smiled? What was there about your personality that sparked the betrayal? And is there something about you that might spark a new betrayal? Is it any wonder that the question persists, "Do you love me?"

Little wonder, then, as Jesus stood facing Peter, that he asked three times, "Do you love me?" He too needed to be reassured that he wouldn't be abandoned again. Do you think that Jesus was finally satisfied with Peter's third response? The answer to that question is another question. Is the relationship after a betrayal ever the same? Do any of us retain the same set of assumptions about any relationship after a betrayal? Or are we painfully aware that now betrayal remains a possibility?

Because we are more aware than ever that betrayal is a possibility, the reemergence of trust is a remarkable testimony that in the midst of death, life too is a possibility. Today, then, as we reflect on Jesus' experience of betrayal, let us pray that we shall experience a trust reborn out of the same cross of betrayal that led to Jesus' resurrection.

IV.

Feastday Fanfare

Keeping Sight
of the Familiar

Frequently, preachers spend an unusual amount of time preparing sermons for feastdays. They want their sermons to be special because these days are special. But the efforts at writing better-than-average sermons for these days can backfire, and the results are more sermons to hate. What are some reasons preachers so often find it difficult to preach on feastdays?

One reason is the temptation to dwell in the mythical language of the feast. For example, Christmas sermons abound with allusions to Baby Jesus surrounded by glowing parents, awe-struck shepherds, angels tooting trumpets, and the traveling trio of magi. Easter sermons, on the other hand, are couched in razzle-dazzle resurrection language intended to convince the faithful that Jesus' resurrection is proof positive that doubting Thomases, secular humanists, and atheists ought to be ashamed of themselves. After all, the Holy Shroud alone is sufficient evidence that Jesus had it over Houdini!

Another reason feastday preaching is difficult is that many of the names of the feastdays are mystifying. If the congregation doesn't even understand why they are

116

congregating, it's no wonder preachers struggle writing sermons. For example, what comes to mind when the Feast of The Immaculate Conception is mentioned? Educated Catholics think twice before answering and when they do they're not certain the conception in question refers to Mary or Jesus. The word "immaculate" sounds more like an adjective associated with a clean wash rather than a salvific event. And what about the Feast of The Assumption? Mary's assumption, of course! We all have assumptions—about our lives, our spouses, our friends, and our work. So what's Mary's assumption? Then there is the feast of The Annunciation. The annunciation to Mary, of course! I bet some people think the feast is the feast of The Enunciation, not The Annunciation. How many people get any kind of an annunciation in their lives? "The other day I received an annunciation and let me tell you...."

The bigger-than-life associations with feastdays, as well as the mystifying titles so many feastdays have, make it difficult for the preacher to speak about the human experience these feastdays celebrate. Many preachers are more inclined to appropriate the inflated celebratory language of the feast and inflate it even more. No wonder preachers work overtime preparing feastday sermons.

Once more, preachers need to remind themselves that the focus in preaching needs to be on the human experience being celebrated. Concentrating on what is deeply human in the event can, paradoxically, lead the congregation to discover something richly fulfilling and truly worthy of calling for the praise and thanksgiving on those days we call feasts.

Christmas

The Fleshy Way
of God

John 1:1-18

The Word became flesh and made his dwelling among
us, and we have seen his glory: The glory of an only
Son coming from the Father, filled with enduring
love.

Ah! Today, Christmas day, the words from John's
gospel are an invitation to draw near to the Word made
flesh. In countless countries all over the world, people
are singing carols celebrating the cherubic child in the
manger: "Silent Night, Holy night," "Joy To The World!"
"Angels We Have Heard On High."

Yes, the Word was made flesh. But what kind of flesh
do we find in manger scenes or Christmas cards?
Smooth flesh! Unblemished flesh! Scented flesh! Not
only is the child appealing but so too are the other
figures who surround the Word made flesh. Mary,
Joseph, the shepherds, angels, even the animals come in
Camay cleaned-up flesh! We feel so comfortable in their

presence. We are delighted to be in the company of the Word made flesh. Who wouldn't want to associate with this Word?

We don't need to look far. John tells us in verse eleven that the "Word came to what was his own, but his own people did not accept him." His own people did not accept him? How could this be? It doesn't make sense! Why would anyone turn from the Word made flesh? The radiant Madonna with child is so compelling that it doesn't seem possible anyone could turn away.

Could it be that his own people didn't accept him precisely because what they encountered was the Word made *fleshy*, not flesh? The Word made fleshy? Put that way, we, too, might have a difficult time accepting the Word, whereas we are delighted to embrace the Word made flesh!

What is the fleshy Word?

Have you ever seen the charred flesh of burn victims?

Have you ever seen the blotched flesh of people with AIDS?

Have you felt wrinkled flesh?

Have your eyes ever lingered on varicose-veined flesh? Arthritic flesh?

Cataracted flesh?

Have you ever noticed the smell and sweat of fevered flesh?

It's no wonder that we prefer the Word made flesh to the Word made fleshy. Ironically, what we really want is flesh that isn't really flesh. We prefer the sanitized, transparent, angelic flesh. What we adore and gush over are the scrubbed, beaming, beautiful, bronze gods on television. We are in awe of the superdressed, superbuilt, and superhuman. So what's wrong with dressing up the manger with department store mannequins?

But the Word was made fleshy. God draws near in a fleshy way. Jesus is the fleshy way of God. Yes, God does come in varicose veins and cataracts. The fleshy God is there coughing up sputum. And we are reminded that when God speaks it is in a fleshy, human way—that is, sputtering and stammering words of love or pain or joy or sorrow.

We are further reminded that when we press the flesh, touch, or are touched, God is there in a fleshy way touching and being touched.

Today more than any other day, we need to remind ourselves how the Word does and doesn't draw near to us. For the temptation is to think we have accepted the Word made flesh when we have actually accepted an angelic word, an other-worldly word. Today more than any other day, we need to profess wholeheartedly our belief in the Word made flesh, the fleshy Word of God.

God's
Hallmark

John 1:1-18

In the beginning was the Word; the Word was in God's
presence, and the Word was God. He was present to
God in the beginning. Through him all things came
into being, and apart from him nothing came to be.

*W*e celebrate the birth of Christ today, but the gospel
reading is the first chapter from John. Doesn't it seem
strange that we would be listening to a reading about
God's Word coming into the world rather than hearing
the familiar story of Jesus' birth in a manger? What
possible appeal can a reading about a word have, even if
it is The Word, God's Word?

I think we can begin to appreciate John's word about
The Word, "In the beginning was the Word," by
recalling one of the activities that engages most of us
before Christmas. I am referring to our buying and
selling Christmas cards.

Buying Christmas cards can be a real expense, especially if we have lots of relatives, friends, and acquaintances to whom we intend to send them. Not only do we have the cost of the cards to consider but we also have to take into account the cost of postage. As we review the names of the persons on our Christmas list, we probably are going to send the more inexpensive cards to people whom we know but who are not close friends. The message on these cards is simple and uniform: "Merry Christmas!" "Have a Happy Holiday!" We reserve the better cards for closer friends, and the message might be a little more personal. And we are willing to spend more money on the people who are close to us. How close?

Those whom we care enough to send the very best! I am indebted to Hallmark Cards for this line, although I am not plugging Hallmark Cards. What the "very best" means is that we are searching for the card that expresses exactly how we feel about our mother or father, spouse or lover. If I am going to put out a buck or two for a card, then the words on that card are going to express me to a T. And when the person I love gets the card, that person will say, "Boy, I could have guessed who'd send a card like this! It's just like him!" The person recognizes the words and the design as something I alone would send—the card was my hallmark!

What does this have to do with the first chapter in John's gospel? Simply this. When John speaks about the Word as coming from God, I think he is telling us that God cared enough to send the very best! God wanted to express exactly how he felt about us and realized not just any word would do. No, God wanted the one word that conveyed his passion for us, and therefore chose to send the Word. Jesus is God's special Word, his Hallmark! Nothing cheap about God! If this alone were the message in John's gospel, we would have much to ponder and be thankful about. However, John tells us something very startling. He says "All things came to be through him, and without him nothing came to be." Now that is good news!

All of us have come to be through the Word. This means that each of us is a word from and through the Word. And because we have come to be through the Word, we aren't cheap words or dirty words. I get the impression from talking to some people that they don't think much of themselves; they don't value who they are. Unfortunately, preachers in the pulpit and on TV often preach how sinful we are, but they fail to remind us that we are fundamentally good words coming from the hand of God. Today we are reminded who we are. We, too, are the hallmark of God. We too are sent to one another through God's Word, God's Hallmark.

That we are *sent* needs to be emphasized. People buy expensive cards to send them to people they love. They do not bring the cards home in order to hide them. They send the cards because cards are meant to be sent. It is that simple. And when cards reach their destination, the people who receive them have their lives brightened even if it is just for the moment. God sent his Word. He did not hide it. He sent it in order to lighten up our lives. That is what John tells us in the gospel.

Since we came to be through this Word, we too are sent to be light-bearing words to one another. We are not meant to be hidden away in the darkness. We are words, words of light, and our being is being sent! If we choose to hide ourselves, then we are denying our identity as words sent to illumine the darkness.

John's message to us is always timely because we frequently lose sight of who we are and what we are called to be. However, his message is particularly appropriate during this season of light. God has sent his Word, his Hallmark, and through our kinship with this Word, we too are words from God, God's hallmarks. We are reminded that he cared enough to send the very best, and that is why we rejoice today, Christmas Day.

Palm Sunday

People
Power

Luke 19:28-40

As he approached Bethphage and Bethany on the
mount called Olivet, he sent two of the disciples with
these instructions: "Go into the village straight ahead
of you. Upon entering it you will find an ass tied there
which no one has yet ridden. Untie it and lead it back.
If anyone should ask you, "'Why are you untying the
beast?' say, 'The Master has need of it.'"

*T*oday we celebrate Palm Sunday. For a number of
years I have wondered how seriously Jesus wants us to
regard his triumphal procession into Jerusalem. I know
that we have taken it very seriously for centuries. Jesus
enters the city and all of his followers wave palm
branches and sing "Hosanna, Hail to the Son of David."
But I have a suspicion that Jesus didn't want us to take
what he was doing all that seriously. In fact, I am
willing to wager that he wanted us to have a moderately
good laugh as we celebrate his entry into the city. Why
do you think he might be asking us to laugh with him

rather than getting carried away by too many Hosannas and Alleluias? I think the answer to that question is found in Jesus' attitude toward anyone who uses power to impress others.

On one occasion when Jesus' disciples were arguing among themselves who was the greatest, Jesus told them that the people he wanted to associate with had to be people who didn't get hung up on who was top banana. He wasn't impressed with people who threw their weight around, especially if it was to demean others. There were enough of those kind already in circulation! What he preferred were persons who used power to empower others. I think we could say that Jesus was interested in people power—that is, in helping people recognize that they had the power to effect changes in their lives. He wasn't interested in putting on the glad rags of power to impress others.

Does it make sense that Jesus would have been serious the day he rode on a donkey into Jerusalem? The fact that he rode a donkey and not a legionnaire's horse indicates that he was gently mocking authority and power as most of us see power. Instead of coming in on an army tank, in other words, he chose to come in on a coaster wagon. Can you imagine someone pulling the pope into town in a wagon? Or asking the President to ride on the front of a bicycle-built-for-two with the First Lady on the back? No, we think that these people need limousines. We think it fits the office. Jesus didn't seem to think a big horse, the equivalent to a bullet-proof limo, suited him. He was satisfied with a donkey, a wagon by our standards.

What does all this mean for us? We like nice clothes, fancy cars, and expensive restaurants. We like class. We don't have royalty, but we treat people in the White House as if they were royalty. We like power. It makes us feel important; it gives us a thrill. We like to:

gun the engine,
give orders from a big desk,
tell people to shut up over a loudspeaker,
write letters dictating how people are to act and not to act,
yell at them,
hold a gun to their heads,
control others through silent power—the passive-aggressive pouting.

Yes, we like power.

But Jesus sends his disciples for a donkey. Then he says to his disciples, "You'll see what I think about authority. I'll ride this donkey. I'll show you that genuine power is people power. Power that empowers and affirms others' abilities! That is what I am about!"

So this celebration sets the tone for the week. We are getting ready to celebrate the last days of Jesus, the one who came to use power, not abuse it. He is the one who took the instrument of torture, an instrument of power, and made of it an expression of love. That is what this week is about.

Good Friday

Silence

Matthew 26:14-27:66

Then toward midafternoon Jesus cried out in a loud
tone, *"Eli Eli, lema sabachtani?"*, that is, "My God,
my God, why have you forsaken me?"

*J*esus felt betrayed three times before he died. We can
imagine what he must have felt the first two times. He
was betrayed by his disciple Judas and by his friend
and disciple Peter. Jesus anticipated these betrayals, as
we read in the gospel. Judas' and Peter's betrayals he
could understand. Yes, these betrayals hurt him deeply,
but he could comprehend how greed or cowardice or
some other kind of weakness can consume a friend or a
colleague and lead to betrayal. So these betrayals hurt,
but they were intelligible. The third betrayal was
something else!

The first two betrayals must have left Jesus
wondering if he could ever trust anyone. Anyone but
God, the one he called Father. Yes, the first two

betrayals must have left Jesus wondering if deceit ran
so deeply in human nature that he would ever be able to
accomplish what he had set out to do. Still he knew
enough about the human heart not to be totally
overwhelmed by his disciples' betrayal. But the third?
What had that to do with the human heart?

"My God, my God, why have *You* forsaken me?" This
he had not anticipated. Never in a million years could
he have thought that God would let him down, that God
would abandon him. So he cried out to God "Why have
You abandoned me?" But sometimes those who betray
us don't give us answers. They are silent, and we are
left alone in the silence to struggle for an answer. This
is what happened to Jesus. He couldn't comprehend the
way it all ended—on the cross. He couldn't fit this into
the scheme of things. How would he sort this out? He
was betrayed by the one who called him "my beloved." It
didn't make sense! He asked why, and all he got was
silence.

We have some idea of what he must have felt. We
have known betrayals and we have understood why
some of these betrayals have taken place. They continue
to hurt but they are bearable because we understand.
Yet, there are those times when we don't understand.
We are betrayed and there is no answer to our demand
for an explanation. There is nothing but silence. We
want to know why and there is only awful silence. Left
to hang on our crosses, we suffer dumbly, shaking our
heads—waiting for an explanation—and there is only
silence.

Does Jesus get an answer from God? Does the silence
break? Does he finally say,"I see. I understand"? Do
things finally add up or make sense at the end? Well, all

we know from Matthew's gospel is that he cried out in a loud voice and died. And in Luke's gospel, Jesus commends his spirit to the Father. He gets no answer. He simply surrenders to the silence. Jesus places his trust in the Silent One.

Christians celebrate the Feast of the Resurrection as the triumph of the power of being over non-being, of life over death. We believe this is God's response to the one who trusts. We believe the silence is broken in the resurrection. It is God telling us in Jesus that the silence that envelopes us is not death but life, not a curse but a blessing.

But how do we arrive at that discovery? It is for us to struggle with the betrayals that do not yield to answers and discover in the silence what we seek. And the only guarantee we have is our faith that the answer is in Jesus, the risen one.

Easter

Insurrection

John 20:1-9

Early in the morning on the first day of the week, while it was still dark, Mary Magdalene came to the tomb. She saw that the stone had been moved away, so she ran off to Simon Peter and the other disciple (the one Jesus loved) and told them, "The Lord has been taken from the tomb! We don't know where they have put him!"

Of all the days of the year, this is the day we ask ourselves:
Do we really want resurrection life like Jesus?
Do we really want the stones in front of our tombs rolled away as the stones in front of Jesus' tomb were rolled away?
Do we really want release from our burial clothes as Jesus was released from his?
Do we want resurrection garments?
Do we want to share in resurrection glory?

136

Silly questions! Of course we want resurrection life.
Who wouldn't jump at the opportunity? Who wouldn't
be standing in line? Eager to rise up?

After all, resurrection life is reassuring, comforting. If
you've been crying your heart out for someone who's
dying or left you, what you need and want is
resurrection life—some reassurance that you can
continue living, that you have a future.

Or if you've been deeply depressed, felt the weight of
the stone, been abandoned to the darkness, embalmed
in silence, and dried up inside, you want resurrection
life, the glimmer of light, the lifting of the burden, the
glimpse of hope that the night is over. You welcome the
reassurances of resurrection life!

Or maybe you've felt bad about yourself, dug your own
grave, been badmouthing yourself, felt no good and
worthless. Then resurrection life would mean
reassurance that you are OK, not a piece of crap, but a
lovely work of art from the hands of God.

Of course you'd welcome resurrection life! So the
question whether we want resurrection life is a silly
one. Let's not tarry! Let's go find Jesus and ask for
resurrection life!

But wait!

Have we considered all there is to consider about this
resurrection life? Jesus' resurrection is a rising up—for
sure. But maybe it is also an uprising! An uprising?
Hmmm, that's a different story. This is a resurrection
that is an insurrection. When Jesus rose up, was he not
involved in an insurrection resurrection?

Was his uprising a protest against any and all kinds
of oppression?

Against labeling others as kikes, faggots, niggers, spics?

Against ageism: treating people like dirt because they're too old, too young, too middle-aged?

Against sexism: treating people like dirt because of their sex or sexual preference?

Against racism: treating people like second-class citizens because they're not the right color?

Was Jesus' uprising the cry of the broken heart, the sigh that can't be stifled, the refusal to take things sitting down, the protest against anyone trying to keep others in their place?

And if we want the reassurances of resurrection life, does this mean we are also going to be part of his insurrection, part of his uprising against the powers that would destroy others?

That's living dangerously! That's another matter! We want resurrection life, but do we want the insurrection too?

That's something to think about.

Third Sunday after Easter

High
Hopes

Luke 24:13-35

He said to them, "What are you discussing as you go
on your way?" They halted, in distress, and one of
them, Cleopas by name, asked him, "Are you the only
resident of Jerusalem who does not know the things
that went on there these past few days?" He said to
them, "What things?" They said: "All those that had
to do with Jesus of Nazareth, a prophet powerful in
word and deed in the eyes of God and all the people;
how our chief priests and leaders delivered him up to
be condemned to death, and crucified him. We were
hoping that he was the one who would set Israel free."

*H*ave you ever gotten your hopes up, really up, over
something or someone so that everything was riding on
those hopes? If you haven't, then you can't understand
the story of the disciples on the way to Emmaus. High
hopes! That's what they had while Jesus was alive,
these disciples of Jesus. We can imagine them talking

about the high hopes they had as they walked toward
the village of Emmaus.

Jesus would be the one, the winner! They had placed
their bets on him; they had patted one another on the
back. He was their lucky number, their winning ticket.
He would be their dream come true, their liberator. No
doubt about it!

We know the feeling. We understand how excited they
had been as they saw Jesus work the crowds. We can
appreciate their looking at one another and nodding,
"That's my man!" because we know what it's like to
have high hopes. You've had your own dreams. Maybe it
was getting married and there were great expectations.
Or maybe it was your job or career prospects that gave
you high hopes. Perhaps it was a relationship—a
friendship or love affair. High hopes! Possibly it was
high hopes for the children—how smart they would be
or how they'd go places once they left home and were on
their own. Think back to one of those times, and you
will realize what Jesus' disciples had felt when they
admired their man Jesus as he walked and talked with
the people.

Yes, they had high hopes all right, but we know what
happened. It didn't work out as they had hoped. "We
had hoped," they said with a touch of regret and
sadness on their way to Emmaus. But it never works
out as "we had hoped." It never does, does it?

> Something happens,
> something goes wrong,
> something fizzles,
> something gets messed up.

His disciples had hoped, but it all fell through.

High Hopes

No winner here in this man.
All the eggs in the one basket broke.
The dream turned into a nightmare.
He was killed, and he didn't even go out in a blaze of
glory but was unceremoniously nailed to a piece of wood!
Shattered hopes! We know the experience only too
well! The marriage at best is a sparkler, not a skybound
firecracker. It sputters frequently or fizzles out
altogether. We find that friends let us down, don't
understand, or misunderstand. They give us the
runaround. Lovers cheat! The job sucks and our wheels
spin as we go round and round, going nowhere. Then we
retire, get pinned with a cheap imitation gold medal,
and eat an It-was-nice-to-have-you chicken dinner. Yes,
we know what it's like to have high hopes. The kids
move away and have the same problems we had. They
don't write or call home and "thanks" is a word they
haven't learned. What happened? To us? To life?
So we know the feeling of shattered hopes. We know
what those disciples were talking about as they walked
to Emmaus. There was nothing left but an empty tomb.
High hopes, then shattered hopes, and finally
emptiness. Just emptiness. They thought they'd have
everything and they ended up with nothing—Zilch!
Isn't that the way it works out so often? High hopes,
then shattered hopes, and finally emptiness!
A blank!
Zilch!
Zero!
Nothing!
The marriage, the career, the kids, life! So what are
you left with? Well, in the story these disciples sit down
to eat with this stranger. Something ordinary. Eating

142

and breathing. Ordinary indeed. They are with one another and this stranger.

But as they eat and drink with the stranger, they begin to discover that the one they had hoped in, the one they had placed their bets on, the one who let them down and left them with shattered hopes—that very same person was sitting with them even as they talked about how he was nowhere to be found.

Surprise! He was with them, not as they had hoped or dreamed or imagined him to be with them. He was with them in their eating and drinking. Right there he was with them. They had high hopes, then shattered hopes, finally nothing—so they thought. But now he was with them in a new, surprising, totally unexpected way.

Have we ever had our hopes up? Had them shattered? Saw only emptiness? Felt only emptiness? And then, surprise! Found life and companionship in a new way? Have the dead, broken relationships come back in a startling new way ever? Have we come back from the dead in a new way? Have we ever come to discover in the ordinary activity of eating and drinking with others something special and wonderful that we had not expected or anticipated? Have our hearts not been lifted up unexpectedly after we had lost all and had our hopes dashed?

Is that what this story is about?

143

Ascension

Looking in the
Right Place

Acts 1:1-11

> They were still gazing up into the heavens when two
> men dressed in white stood beside them. "Men of
> Galilee," they said, "why do you stand here looking
> up at the skies? This Jesus who has been taken from
> you will return, just as you saw him go up into the
> heavens."

"Why are you looking off into space? Haven't you got
anything better to do?" The angels didn't phrase it quite
that way the day Jesus bade farewell to his friends. But
when his friends anxiously scanned the heavens for
some sign of his presence, the angels urged them to
redirect their attention elsewhere. Why had Jesus'
friends been so anxious?

Recall who Jesus was to his friends. He was their
leader, a charismatic leader by most anybody's
standards. He attracted the crowds through his
preaching. He was compassionate and courageous.
Given his attendance at so many parties, he must have

been highly extroverted. However, he also cherished moments of solitude. At home with people from all strata of Jewish society, Jesus was most certainly admired by his disciples. Because he was their Master, they looked to him not only as the one who embodied the qualities I have described, but also as the one who provided direction.

No small wonder that when he bade them farewell he left a terrible void in their hearts. We can get a sense of that vacuum if we think about our own experiences that correspond with theirs. Undoubtedly we have known or lived with persons who had considerable talents and dynamic personalities. If any of us had an intelligent, caring spouse whose insight we cherished, and if that spouse suddenly died, we can understand the disciples' problem. Even if a friend were not so intelligent or caring, if that person embodied any enviable quality and that person moved away or left us, we would understand the disciples' dilemma.

Implicit in what I have described is that by admiring qualities belonging exclusively to others, we can never acknowledge those same qualities in ourselves. For example, we could admire another's courage or celebrate a friend's wit or sense of humor but never dream that we too might possess those same qualities—at least not while the other person had such a commanding presence in our lives.

If the Ascension means anything, it means that Jesus had to depart; he couldn't continue doing business as usual. Only by his departure could his disciples discover within themselves that they too were able to do what Jesus had done in his ministry. They needed to experience Jesus' loss in one way in order to reexperience his presence in a new way. And that new way was Jesus' gift of the Spirit. After the Ascension had taken place, the angels asked the disciples why they continued to gaze heavenward. The angels' simple message was that Jesus would be back with them. This message the disciples would discover in the days, weeks, and months that followed, when Jesus had returned in his Spirit. Through the power of this Spirit, they would become aware of and develop abilities they thought only Jesus possessed.

Gazing heavenward is a way of describing any one of us when we don't recognize that what we are looking for "out there" is within. Searching the horizon, we wait and wait for someone's return. We don't get anything done; we are immobilized. We are depressed and we grieve the loss of a person who meant so much to us.

But I believe that we have our own angels who appear during times of grieving; these angels present themselves as our own questions. "Why are you looking into space? Don't you know that things have to be done? They aren't going to take care of themselves!" When we pay attention to these angels, then I think we can make our own discoveries.

What Jesus' disciples discovered and proclaimed about the special gift called the Spirit is that they too could be compassionate, courageous, and charismatic in their own way as Jesus was in his. I think that many of us need to be reminded that we have received that gift as well. We need not gaze heavenward toward the one who has departed; we need to look within and discover that he is present through our empowerment to be in our way what he was in his.

Pentecost

Spirit
People

Acts 2:1-11

When the day of Pentecost came it found them gathered in one place. Suddenly from up in the sky there
came a noise like a strong, driving wind which was
heard all through the house where they were seated.
Tongues as of fire appeared, which parted and came
to rest on each of them. All were filled with the Holy
Spirit.

*S*piritual! Today we celebrate Pentecost—the feast of
the Spirit giving birth to sons and daughters. Today we
are challenged to be persons of the spirit—spiritual!

Is this an inviting challenge?

Does it turn you on?

Make you excited?

Get your blood going?

Rev your motor?

Spiritual! Would you be on cloud nine if you
overheard a friend say about you, "Hey, you want to go
out on a date with someone spiritual? Well, I have just

the right person in mind! I can't tell you what a great spiritual evening you have in store for you!" Or, "How would you like to play a game of craps with a real spiritual dude? You're in for a treat. Let me tell you about my friend!"

Spiritual! Yeah, man, the call to be spiritual is as inviting as eating spinach—maybe necessary, but not very appetizing! Let's face it! When someone says we should be spiritual, it's like saying we should go to the dentist! We gotta do it, but... So, unless we figure out why the challenge to be spiritual sounds so uninviting, we won't be able to celebrate this feast at all.

What's the problem? The problem is we already have some negative ideas of what it means to be spiritual.

"She's so spiritual"—meaning otherworldly! Upturned eyes, folded hands, never walks but glides across the room! We are talking about a meek, mild-mannered mannequin—a space cadet not in touch with the here and now. This person talks about God and religion morning, noon, and night, and quotes the Bible every five minutes. She puts just about everybody to sleep in the process!

"He's so spiritual"—meaning restrained! This person doesn't raise his voice, doesn't swear, doesn't sweat, doesn't get worked up, doesn't put his foot in his mouth, doesn't make booboos, doesn't eat too much, doesn't drink too much, doesn't laugh too loud, doesn't tell off-color jokes, doesn't bother the neighbors. This person is controlled, sober, careful, well behaved—very spiritual!

"She's so spiritual"—meaning passive or wimpy! She looks like she's sitting on a tack! She is long-, very long-suffering, patient, willing to wait forever for things to change! Doesn't complain! Takes it on the chin! She is self-sacrificing (and shows it), and modest—oh, so modest! "Aw shucks, folks, what I did was nothing! I'm nobody!"

Is this what it means to be spiritual? Otherworldly? Restrained? Passive? If that's what it means, then I'd say being spiritual means being *boring!* This kind of a person you don't need at a party! This kind you need when you want to get to sleep in a hurry! What, then, do we mean when we speak of being spiritual? I think we begin to get an answer when we turn to the first reading for this feast.

In the Acts of the Apostles, we read that after Jesus died, his friends gathered in a second-story room where they frequently met when Jesus was alive. Now they were scared, scared as hell! Frightened out of their minds. Why? Well, Jesus had been the boss, the leader, the rock, the comforter, the one to whom they had always turned for the answers to their questions. Now they were alone like widowers or widows, like orphans. Think how they felt! Think how you'd feel. Think how you've felt when someone close has left the scene. "Who are we? We're nobodies! Just fishermen, has-beens! What can we do? Stay inside; that's what we'll do! Play it safe! Protect ourselves! Curl up and die!" Oh yes, we know the feeling!

So they barred the doors! Drew the blinds on the windows! Stared glumly at one another! Thumped their fingers on the table! Moaned, groaned, and quaked in their boots! For hours on end.

But then it happened! Something somewhere in that room began to stir! Breathing, light breathing! Hardly noticeable at first! Then the breathing got louder and it

sounded like a wind swirling about! Woooooo! Wooooo!
Woooooo! And that wind filled the room, enveloping
everybody and everything in sight! And lo and behold!
   Jesus' friends stopped thumping their fingers on the
table,

> stopped moaning, groaning, and quaking in
> their boots,
> stopped bad-mouthing and nay-saying
> themselves to death,
> and they began smiling!

They knew something wonderful had happened. They
sprang to their feet, marched to the windows and doors,
and flung them open to the blue of sky! Then they came
down to earth, to the marketplace people! From the
upper room they came down and gossiped joyfully,
clearly, loudly, what they believed! God's Spirit was a-
percolating in them! Bubbling up! Up! Up!
   Those who heard were amazed! At first they thought
Jesus' friends were drunk. Filled with booze! The
disciples laughed! It was only nine in the morning—too
early for martinis and Bloody Mary's were as yet
non-existent (though there was a Holy Mary on the
scene). No, they weren't filled with the spirits we call
booze, but with The Spirit! And what did the Spirit do
to them?
   Well now, we are getting an answer to our question
about what it means to be spiritual. They became people
of the earth—earthy people. They became freed-up
people, freed from the restraints that burden the spirit!
They became actively engaged in life! Not passive
puppets but earth people! Freed-up people! Involved
people! That's what it means to be spiritual!

Spiritual! Of this world, earthly. That's the paradox!
To be spiritual is to be grounded, earthy, standing on
the soil. Feet planted firmly on the ground, the spiritual
person doesn't put on airs, doesn't pretend to be what he
or she isn't! The earthy person isn't afraid to get messed
up in the soil of life—yours or anyone else's. The earthy
person is in touch with him- or herself, with you, with
where it's at! With where you're at! The earthy person
hugs you, embraces you! The earthy person celebrates
life with you whether you are twenty, thirty, forty, or
eighty; black or white; straight or gay; single, married,
divorced, remarried, re-divorced. The earthy person will
dance the waltz with you when you want to waltz; the
polka when you want to polka; the foxtrot when you
want to foxtrot. But the earthy person will challenge
you to dance the waltz when all you want to do is dance
the polka all the days of your life or will challenge you
to do the foxtrot when all you want to do is waltz away
your life, or get you to dance in the dance of life when
all you want to do is rock away your life in the corner of
a room.

Spiritual means being freed up! Freed up from and
freed up for! Freed up from the tie-me-downs, the
paralyses of the spirit, the things that weigh us down
and keep us from becoming what God wants us to
become. Being spiritual keeps you from saying you're
too old or too young or not educated or of no worth.

The spiritual person who is freed up is convinced he
or she is of worth and value in the eyes of God and can
bring God's light and love into the lives of others.

Spiritual means being engaged; it means being active
rather than passive or wimpy. This means being
passionate, caring, risking, reaching out. Being engaged

means not being a bystander, a spectator. It means being in the parade, drumming the drums. To be engaged means not waiting for the kingdom day to come but bringing it about! The spiritual person takes the initiative and opens the doors and windows rather than waiting around for someone else to open them.

Yes, the spiritual person is this: worldly, freed up, and engaged. Spiritual! The challenge is there! Through our birth at Pentecost we are called to become what we are: sons and daughters of the Pentecost Spirit!

Body of Christ

You're Nobody Till
Somebody Loves You

Mark 14:12-16, 22-26

During the meal he took bread, blessed and broke it,
and gave it to them. "Take this," he said, "this is my
body.

"You're Nobody Till Somebody Loves You." Have you
ever stopped to consider why this song title does or
doesn't make sense? Is it true that you're nobody till
somebody loves you? What better time to wrestle with
the question than today, the feast of the Body of Christ?
Before we can answer the question, we have to consider
what we mean by "nobody," by "somebody," and while
we are at it, by "anybody."

We've all had the experience of being a nobody. You
walk down the street and nobody recognizes you. It is as
though you never existed. You go to a party and nobody
knows you. You try to engage someone in conversation
and the person says, "Excuse me! I see a friend of mine
in the other room." You look over to see there are no

people in the other room! So you spend half the evening deciding what kind of cracker you want with your pickled herring. You feel like a nobody. People don't even ask "Who's that over there?" because if you are a nobody, you aren't even visible. Most of us experience being a nobody some time or other.

I sit at home on a Sunday afternoon and no one calls; I'm nobody.

I'm set up for a blind date and the person doesn't show up; I'm nobody.

I pour my heart out to someone and the person yawns and says, "What was that?"

I have little money in the bank; I'm nobody.

I'm out of work and can't find a job; I'm nobody.

I live in a dreary one-room flat with a lumpy mattress, chipped plates, and a broken-down couch; I'm nobody.

I look in the mirror and what do I see? A nobody.

Most of us know what it's like to be a nobody sometime or other. But some folk know what it's like to be nobodies all the time:

> people in nursing homes, rocking away their lives, nobodies whom nobody visits,
> elderly folk who might have been somebodies but are now forever nobodies shuffling down the streets,
> people with AIDS who feel like nobodies because their friends and relatives have deserted them,
> little kids abandoned emotionally by parents who never notice them feeling like nobodies.

Of course no one wants to be a nobody. So, from time to time people get desperate and do wild things to attract others' attention just to let them know they aren't nobodies. People feeling like nobodies often commit suicide, saying in effect, "You thought I was a nobody; well, I will take my life and now that I am gone, you will regard me as having been a somebody." Pretty drastic, wouldn't you say?

And then there are the anybodies. They are a step up from being nobodies. They are noticed. And why? Because they are functionaries. They perform a service; they fill slots. They are cooks or cab drivers or ministers or teachers or dentists or secretaries or moms or dads. You notice them for what they do. That, however, is the only reason they are noticed. They may be good at what they do and thousands upon thousands of people say of an anybody, "Wow he does good work! What would we do without him? People like him are irreplaceable!" Oh yeah?

Anybodies can be replaced at what they do, and when they are sick or die we replace them with anybody else who can do what they did. So we refer to people who fill slots as anybodies. Anybodies come and go. When one anybody leaves, another is there to take his or her place.

Finally, there are somebodies. A somebody is someone I notice and like because I find that person unique. It is the *you* in the somebody I notice, love, and admire. Not *what you* do, but *you*. You may be a bumbling, inefficient anybody, not too great in the slot you fill. But that doesn't matter to someone who loves you. You are special to that person. All of you, I hope, know what it is like to be liked because you are you—warts and beauty marks alike.

Now, it may be that no one has noticed the *you* in you—has not acknowledged that you are a

recognized some of the numbers who comes at like ...
boasting, biting,

[handwritten: OlD spice + Mus u OlD salts & Noes]

somebody—and that is sad. Why? Because you end up
feeling like a nobody when you are really somebody! Ah!
That's it! We have an answer to the question we posed
at the beginning. You are nobody till somebody loves
you!

Actually, you are always somebody, but until someone
notices the *you* in the somebody, you end up feeling like
a nobody. That's a tragedy because there's something
about each person that is unique, waiting to be
revealed. And unless what is unique or special about
the person is discovered, then another fantastic
discovery won't happen. What is that great discovery?
We find that answer in this Feast of The Body of Christ.

When we really see in someone a special "you," a deep
connection is revealed. This is what we mean when we
speak about belonging to the Body of Christ. When we
wake up to the fact that there is in all people a special
quality that makes them somebodies, we also discover
that they have God's blood running through their veins;
they have God's breath in their lungs; God's heart in
their chest.

Of course, none of this realization can dawn until we
reverse the trend of treating individuals and classes of
people like nobodies, and other people like just
anybodies. We must first see people as they are, as
somebodies. People out of work; women in the church;
children growing up; the homeless; the poor among us.
They are all somebodies, not nobodies. Only when we
understand this is it possible for us to celebrate the fact
that we are all from God, all God's body, the body of
Christ.

[handwritten: s hire that loot of Chrish ~ lord go hab mne me ke]

[handwritten: potential noshd / overly sensited to certon / sit bord - wont drop stern nets / Certin nts stern 161 / hb.]

Christ the King

Crowning
Achievement

John 18:33-37

"My kingdom does not belong to this world. If my
kingdom were of this world, my subjects would be
fighting to save me from being handed over to the
Jews. As it is, my kingdom is not here."

*T*oday is the feast of Christ the King. Is there anybody
in the congregation who has lost any sleep waiting for
this feastday? I don't think many of us find this feast
holds much meaning, and the reason is obvious. We
don't live in a monarchy. True, presidents enjoy pomp
and pageantry, and we accord them accolades ordinarily
reserved for monarchs. But the monarchy doesn't hold
the same fascination today that it once did. Not that we
have anything against monarchs like Baudoin of
Belgium, Elizabeth of England, or Juan Carlos of Spain.
They are nice people; we admire them. But that is as far
as it goes. And given the presence of despotic rulers in
the world, I think we'd prefer that monarchs keep their

Crowning Achievement

distance. But we still have to come to terms with this
feast. What can we do to appreciate Jesus as king?

I have an idea I'd like you to think about. Bear with
me because you'll think I'm a little insane as I develop
it, but eventually I think you'll see the point I want to
make. Let's spend a little time thinking about how we
use the word "king" in our conversations. We speak of
the lion as the king of the beasts and we have all heard
of King Kong, a powerful but much maligned oversized
gorilla. And the Schlitz people boast that theirs is the
king of beer. Of course anyone old enough in this
congregation knows of the late Wayne King, the waltz
king. If you want a great burger you go to Burger King.
And as you eat it you might want to listen to Bobby
Vinton, the Polish Prince, belt out the Beer Barrel
Polka. OK, OK, so he's not a king! But he is royalty, isn't
he? Then there's that old cowboy, Roy Rogers, king of
the cowboys, and there's a lesser known king, the polka
king, Frankie Yankovitch, who still reigns somewhere
in Wisconsin. But enough is enough! What is the point
in rattling off a list of kings as varied as the hamburger
king and the waltz king?

As we listen to the list, we realize that however
diverse, all these kings share something in
common—they excel at what they do. They all have
some crowning achievement. For example, the lion has
a roar that would frighten anyone, and King Kong made
the earth tremble when he beat his hairy chest. Schlitz
claimed it had the best beer and Burger King the best
burgers in the land. You could waltz your way to the
stars with Wayne King, and laugh till your sides split
with Alan King! And our friend the Polish Prince could
shame any kingly pretender with "Roll Out the Barrel!"

Crowning Achievement

Today we celebrate Christ as a king. What does he
excel at? What's his crowning achievement? Well, we
know what he wasn't the best at. He wasn't the
best-liked, certainly not by the Scribes or Pharisees; the
best dressed (a one-piece tunic and that was it); the
best-looking (nowhere do we read he looked like
Charleton Heston looking like Jesus); the best-likely to
succeed (the cross did not hold the sweet smell of
success); the best-behaved (sweet, simple Jesus he was
not).

Well, then, how did he excel? What was he best at? He
excelled at being human. If you want to know what it is
like to be a powerful gorilla, you look to King Kong; if
you want to know what it is like to be a polka king, you
look to Frankie Yankovitch; if you want to know what it
is like to be human, you look to Jesus.

But what does Jesus excelling at being human mean?
I'd say it means three things:

You count!

I'm for you!

Come to the party!

Over and over in word and deed, Jesus of Nazareth let
it be known that "You count," "I'm for you," "Come to
the party."

"You count!" We know what it means not to count. It
means to be:

> looked through,
> overlooked,
> underlooked,
> nobody,
> a no account,
> nothing.

[handwritten: affirm, make stronger inner a-firm)]

"You count!" This means:

    all the runny noses matter,
    all the overweights matter,
    all the underweights matter,
    all the just-so's matter,
    all the wallflowers, confused, questioning,
    dropouts matter. *[handwritten: divorced, doubting]*

Jesus made everybody feel they counted. He made little Zacchaeus feel ten feet tall. He named Simple Simon "the rock." He turned the prostitute into Dulcinea.

Secondly, Jesus let everybody know, "I'm for you!" Period! Not "I'm for you..."

[handwritten: life together, stay strong, chp gum transmied]

[handwritten: delight me of in diversity his support]

    ...if you pass a test,
    ...if you get your hair cut and your nails cleaned,
    ...if you get smart and well-mannered,
    ...if you get the earring removed,
    ...if you're tops in everything.

No, "I'm for you" as you are, warts and all, neuroses and all. You can rely on me, lean on me, trust me. I'm no fair- weather friend. I believe in you!

Thirdly, Jesus invited everybody to the party. No one was to be:

        excluded,
        rejected,
        turned back,
        cast out,
        sent on their way, refused admittance.

His parties were not:

mutual admiration societies,
elitist gatherings,
old boys' club meetings.

"Come to the party": whites, blacks, browns, polka
dots, men, women, poor, rich, tall, short, old, young,
suburbanites, city folk, country dwellers! You are all
welcome!

Christ's message was and is: "You count, I'm for you,
and come to the party." But what about his crowning
achievement? The touch of glory? His crowning
achievement was and is the cross. No big roar. No polka.
No waltz. No razzle-dazzle on the tennis court. Just the
cross.

Certainly the cross represents others' attempts to cut
short and put an end to Jesus' message. But it is also
Jesus' way of saying you can't stop a winner, a king. He
went all the way to put himself on the line for us, and
he made his point most eloquently on the cross. Because
on that cross he said to another reject: "You count; I'm
for you; this day you will be with me at a party!"

You can't keep a good man down! Long live the king!

split rejection · sin
unfairness of life
suffering of the innocent

Lectionary
References

Cycle A

Scripture	Day of the Year	Story
Matthew 26:14-27:66	Passion Sunday	"Silence"
John 10:1-10	4th Sunday after Easter	"Sheep or Shepherd? "The Good Shepherdess"
Matthew 5:1-12	4th Sunday of the Year	"Consider the Source"
Matthew 18:21-25	24th Sunday of the Year; Tuesday of the 3rd Week in Lent	"How Many Times?"

Cycle B

Scripture	Day of the Year	Story
Genesis 22:1-18	2nd Sunday of Lent	"Voice of God"
Mark 14:12-16, 22-26	Body Of Christ	"You're Nobody Till Somebody Loves You"
John 15:1-8	5th Sunday after Easter	Who Needs Whom?"
Mark 3:20-35	10th Sunday of the Year	"Family Man"
Luke 12:35-38	19th Sunday of the Year; Tuesday of the 29th Week of the Year	"Be Prepared"
Mark 7:14-23	22nd Sunday of the Year; Wednesday of the 5th Week	"Winning Our Way into the Heart of God"
Mark 4:35-40	12th Sunday of the Year	"Somehow"
Mark 6:1-6	14th Sunday of the Year	"You're Just Too Good To Be True"
Mark 8:27-33	24th Sunday of the Year	"Necessary Obstacles"

Cycle C

Scripture	Day of the Year	Story
Luke 4:1-13	1st Sunday of Lent	"God's Pride and Joy"
John 13:31-35	5th Sunday after Easter	"Moment of Glory"
John 13:31-35	5th Sunday after Easter	"Fully Alive— The Kicker
Luke 10:25-37	15th Sunday of the Year	"Partners"
Luke 13:22-30	21st Sunday of the Year; Wednesday of the 30th Week	"Narrow Door"

Cycles A, B, and C

Scripture	Day of the Year	Story
John 1:1-18	Christmas Day	"The Fleshy Way of God"
		"Do You Know What I Mean?"
		"God's Hallmark"
Luke 19:28-40	Palm Sunday	"People Power"
Joel 2:12-18	Ash Wednesday	"A Matter of Heart"
John 20:1-9	Easter	"Insurrection"

Lectionary References

John 20:19-31	2nd Sunday after Easter	"Doubts That Damn and Doubts That Save"
Luke 24:13-35	3rd Sunday after Easter Wednesday of the Octave of Easter	"High Hopes"
Acts 1:1-11	The Ascension	"Downward Mobility?"
		"Looking in the Right Place"
Acts 2:1-11	Pentecost	"Spirit People"
John 21:15-19	Sts. Peter and Paul (Vigil)	"Blessed Assurance"
John 18:33-37	Christ The King	"Crowning Achievement"
Mark 4:1-20	Wednesday of the 3rd Week of the Year	"Going To Seed"
		"Is There Dirt in The Kingdom?"

Other Books by Andre Papineau

BREAKTHROUGH:
Stories of Conversion
Paperbound, $7.95, 139 pages, 5½ x 8½
ISBN 0-89390-128-8

Here is an essential resource for RCIA, cursillo, and renewal programs. You and your group will witness what takes place inside Papineau's characters as they change. These stories will remind you that change, ultimately, is a positive experience. Following each section, you'll find reflections from a psychological point of view, which will help you help others deal with their personal conversions.

JESUS ON THE MEND:
Healing Stories for Ordinary People
Paperbound, $7.95, 150 pages, 5½ x 8½
ISBN 0-89390-140-7

You know that everybody, at some time, needs to heal or be healed. Here are eighteen Gospel-based stories that illustrate four aspects of healing: Acknowledging the Need, Reaching Out for Help, The Healer's Credentials, and The Healer's Therapy. Also included are helpful reflections following each story, which focus on the process of healing taking place.

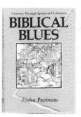

BIBLICAL BLUES:
Growing through Setups and Letdowns
Paperbound, $7.95, 160 pages, 5½ x 8½
ISBN 0-89390-157-1

This book of biblical stories acknowledges the way people set themselves up for letdowns. Papineau reveals Jesus as the ever-playful one who often enters the scene to puncture a balloon, a deflating event that somehow leads to spiritual growth.

Order from your local bookseller, or use the order form on the last page.

More Resources for Preaching

STORY AS A WAY TO GOD:
A Guide for Storytellers

H. *Maxwell Butcher*
Paperbound, $9.95, 153 pages, 5½ x 8½
ISBN 0-89390-201-2

Why are stories so powerful? This book reveals the dynamics of good storytelling. Find out why every good story—from *The Ugly American* to *West Side Story*—says something about the divine. Learn how to find God's story in the Bible and elsewhere. Explore four different ways to tell God's story.

STORYTELLING STEP BY STEP

Marsh Cassady
Paperbound, $9.95, 156 pages, 5½ x 8½
ISBN 0-89390-183-0

The author, a storyteller and drama instructor, takes you through all the steps in telling stories: selecting the right story for you, selecting the right story for your audience, adapting your story for different occasions, analyzing it so that you can present it well, preparing your audience, and, finally, presenting your story. Includes many sample stories.

CREATING STORIES FOR STORYTELLING

Marsh Cassady
Paperbound, $9.95, 144 pages, 5½ x 8½
ISBN 0-89390-205-5

This book picks up where *Storytelling Step by Step* leaves off. Find out how to get ideas to create your own original stories, adapt stories to different audiences, plot a story, create tension, and write dialogue to keep your listeners on the edge of their chairs.

Order from your local bookseller, or use the order form on the last page.

More Story-Sermons...

...from Lou Ruoff

For Give: Stories of Reconciliation
Paperbound, $8.95, 120 pages, 5½ x 8½
ISBN 0-89390-198-9

Great for homily ideas, catechesis, or re-membering church sessions.

No Kidding, God, Where Are You?
Parables of Ordinary Experience
Paperbound, $7.95, 106 pages, 5½ x 8½
ISBN 0-89390-141-5

Twenty-five stories that work best as homilies; to help you with your planning, they are accompanied by Scripture references according to the season of the liturgical year.

...from James Henderschedt

The Light in the Lantern:
True Stories for Your Faith Journey
Paperbound, $8.95, 124 pages, 5½ x 8½
ISBN 0-89390-209-8

Use these stories for personal reflection, homily preparation, or small-group work.

The Topsy-Turvy Kingdom:
More Stories for Your Faith Journey
Paperbound, $7.95, 122 pages, 5½ x 8½
ISBN 0-89390-177-6

Use these twenty-one stories for preaching—they're keyed to the lectionary—or use them in religious education.

The Magic Stone
and Other Stories for the Faith Journey
Paperbound, $7.95, 95 pages, 5½ x 8½
ISBN 0-89390-116-4

Share these stories aloud and the word comes to life for your congregation, prayer group, or adult education classes.

Order from your local bookseller, or use the order form on the last page.

More Story-Sermons... (cont'd)

...from Joseph Juknialis

Angels to Wish By: A Book of Story-Prayers

Paperbound, $7.95, 136 pages, 6 x 9
ISBN 0-89390-051-6

Though a delight to read as a collection of stories, this book is best suited for use in preparing liturgies and paraliturgical celebrations.

A Stillness without Shadows

Paperbound, $7.95, 75 pages, 6 x 9
ISBN 0-89390-081-8

Ten stories for use in church, in school, or at home.

When God Began in the Middle

Paperbound, $7.95, 101 pages, 6 x 9
ISBN 0-89390-027-3

Fourteen more story-prayers illustrating how God comes to us in the middle of our successes, failures, fears, happiness.

Winter Dreams and Other Such Friendly Dragons

Paperbound, $7.95, 87 pages, 6 x 9
ISBN 0-89390-010-9

These fifteen stories remind us that winter prepares for new life, offers the gifts of anticipation and preparation, and conceals blessings yet to be discovered.